48.40

D0962020

FOR REFERENCE
Do Not Take
From This Room

Stories of
The World's Holidays

BY
GRACE HUMPHREY

1924
MILTON BRADLEY COMPANY
SPRINGFIELD, MASSACHUSETTS

Republished by Omnigraphics • Penobscot Building • Detroit • 1990

This is a facsimile reprint of the
1923 edition published in Springfield,
Massachusetts by the Milton Bradley
Company.

Library of Congress Cataloging-in-Publication Data

Humphrey, Grace, 1882-
    Stories of the world's holidays / by Grace Humphrey.
        p.   cm.
    Originally published: Springfield, Mass. : Milton Bradley, 1924.
    Summary: Explains the origin of twenty holidays of various
countries.
    ISBN 1-55888-882-9 (lib. bdg. : alk. paper)
    1. Holidays—Juvenile literature.   [1. Holidays.]   I. Title.
GT3933.H86   1990
394.2'6—dc20   89-43336
                                                                                  CIP
                                                                                  AC

⊗

This book is printed on acid-free paper meeting the ANSI Z39.48
Standard. The infinity symbol that appears above indicates that the
paper in this book meets that standard.

PRINTED IN THE UNITED STATES OF AMERICA

To
MARIA

CONTENTS

CONTENTS

Stories of the World's Holidays

THE MAN IN GRAY

THE NINETEENTH OF JANUARY

Was he right or was he wrong?

The old captain straightened up after placing the wreath at the base of the Lee statue. That puzzling question flashed into his mind again. The crowd was breaking up and leaving. The group of men in gray, the Richmond camp of the United Confederate Veterans, were saying their goodbyes. The captain walked back a few steps and gazed up at the statue.

Was he right or was he wrong?

The last of the old soldiers were hobbling over to the street-car. Fewer of them than last year—the colonel sick, old Jim laid up with rheumatism, Bill gone, Jackson gone too. He looked back to the statue and saluted as he turned away.

The spring of '61, he thought, and its crisis
—was there ever such a tangle of duties and
loyalties?—such a criss-cross of good and evil?
The war's farther and farther away.   State's
rights, secession from the Union, slavery,
things that were all mixed up then seem
maybe clearer now.   The whole's greater than
a part even if that part's the South—yes, even
if it's Virginia.   But there's one thing never
changes—you don't call it change when it
gets deeper and stronger—our love for Marse
Robert.

Yet when a man—not a youngster like us,
but an older, thoughtful man who was against
secession—when that man left the Union because Virginia left it, and served his state so
loyally—well, he was true blue—or true gray!
Still—fighting for Virginia was really fighting
for slavery—

Was he right or wrong after all?   Who's
to say?   Settled at last by the fortunes of war
—the two flags flying side by side in Richmond, this mild January day—flying side by
side all through the South for the birthday of
Robert E. Lee—stars and stripes—stars and
bars.

The old man's eyes were bright as he walked

slowly homeward. Stars and stripes, he thought again, stars and bars. He saw nothing of the holiday crowds, of the decorations on every hand. He saw only pictures of long ago—excited scenes of college students enlisting when word came that Sumter had been fired on, that two more states had seceded. He saw the stately portico of Arlington and fancied he heard footsteps up and down, up and down while a weighty decision was being made. He heard cheering as a tall, fine figure in gray on a gray horse came riding down the lines.

Was he right or was he wrong? No, he couldn't have done anything else—how was it Lincoln put it—with firmness in the right as God gave him to see the right—

The captain turned in at his own gate. On the porch was his young friend Randolph with a girl, a stranger.

"So here we are, waiting for you to tell us the real story, your own first-hand story," explained the lad after he had introduced his guest from the North and told about her amazing questions that morning—why was it a holiday? what was that strange flag?

"Sit here, Miss Ellen," the captain bowed

in his courtly fashion, "where you can see the old flag and my picture of Marse Robert,—that's what we always called General Lee. Now what shall I tell you? Not the history of the civil war—you and Randolph'd be quicker with dates and battles than an old fellow like me. My own story you want?

"No, I didn't get into the army at the start—too young. All my friends at college were enlisting—no debate in their minds. But what a difficult decision it was for Lee! He loved the Union, the Lees had helped to make it. He loved his state Virginia, his people had helped make that too. He knew what war was, shorn of its glamour and glory, for he was a colonel in the army. Should he stand by the United States or should he go with Virginia? It was a life-and-death question.

"Lincoln had called for volunteers to march against the South. Virginia would be the first state to be invaded. If Lee remained in the army he'd have to fight against all he loved best in the world. Northern troops coming to drive out his own people and destroy the country? He'd give his life in defending his home. He decided to cast in his lot with the South."

"I remember," interrupted Ellen excitedly. "He walked up and down all night trying to decide. They told us when we were in Washington and went to see Lee's old home—"

"Arlington," put in Randolph.

"He came downstairs," the captain went on with a nod to each of his listeners, "and said to his wife, 'Well, Mary, the question is settled. Here is my letter of resignation from the army.' He never wavered. He never afterward debated the rightness of his course. Indeed years later he said firmly that he'd decide the same way if it were all to do over.

"Do they tell you northern children, in your history class at school, one thing that made the decision harder—or would have made it harder for most men? Do you know, Miss Ellen, that Lincoln sent to Lee to offer him the chief command of the United States army? It was old General Scott, people think, who suggested this to Lincoln. For he admired Lee greatly and had praised his splendid work in the Mexican war. Here was a chance for an ambitious soldier who already had to his credit a service of more than thirty years.

" 'No,' was his reply, 'if I owned a million slaves I would cheerfully sacrifice them to the preservation of the Union; but to lift my hand against my own state and people is impossible.   I am a son of Virginia.   I must do as my state does.'

"Dazzling rewards, his career, his fortune, his home itself he sacrificed.   He was too wise not to foresee what the war would bring. He never thought it would be a brief struggle, but warned his wife it might last ten years. Virginia would be the scene of many battles. Arlington would be taken by the enemy.

"What do they teach you up there in the North," the old man asked turning to Ellen suddenly, "about the causes of the war?"

"The civil war," said the girl soberly, "did two things: it freed the slaves and it saved the Union.   A lot of Northerners mixed these two things up, but Lincoln saw them clearly. I've often heard my great-uncles talk about it.   One of them enlisted because he was an abolitionist, the other volunteered to help save the Union.   Don't you remember that speech of Lincoln's?

" 'If I could save the Union without freeing any slaves, I would do it.   And if I could save it by freeing some and leaving others alone, I would also do that. My paramount object is to save the Union, and not either to save or destroy slavery.' "

"M—m," said the captain smiling, "then the North didn't fight to free the slaves? Well, neither were we fighting for slavery. Many of us thought slavery wrong, and that it hurt the whites more than the blacks—Lee said that himself. He had freed his own slaves and those that belonged to his wife were to be freed in '62 according to her father's will. But the slaves that Mrs. Grant inherited were slaves till the emancipation proclamation!

"Why, Miss Ellen, a good many soldiers in our army owned no slaves. Could a cause like slavery be incentive enough to make us march and fight and starve for four years? Could such a cause take an army through the hungry winter of '64? Could it be enough to call out the devotion and patient endurance and splendid heroism that were Lee's and that he passed on to his men?

"No, no, we weren't fighting for slavery. We fought to preserve the right of each state to govern itself with no federal interference. We fought because Virginia was invaded.

We fought on our own soil for our homes. And that was a holy cause, dearer to us than life."

Ellen's eyes were fastened on the old captain who looked fixedly at the photograph of Lee. She saw his hand reach out to touch the faded stars and bars, the flag that was so unfamiliar to her northern eyes, the flag that had stood for so much to the South.

"It's the same devotion, the same loyalty to the flag," she thought recalling the look on her great-grandfather's face as he had talked to her about the war and Lincoln. "Well, neither side can claim a monopoly of courage and devotion. North and South, the best and the bravest were fighting. No wonder it took four long years to win, with such a foe!"

"I joined in May of '62," the captain went on, "so my service in the army of Virginia was exactly the same as Marse Robert's. That first year he was in Richmond organizing our troops, then military adviser to President Davis."

"Jeff Davis?" asked Ellen in a puzzled voice. "Hang Jeff Davis to a—" She wondered why Randolph nudged her.

"Then they gave him the army of northern

Virginia. Lee was—how many years old then? Right, fifty-five, with a splendid record behind him. My uncle had been in his regiment in the Mexican war and used to tell us about him. And one of our neighbors was in the squad of marines that went with him to Harper's Ferry to capture John Brown.

"Ah, that brings a flash across your face, Miss Ellen. I suppose today the North feels about that raid much as we do—that it was a wild, crazy scheme, sure to fail or sure to cause endless trouble? The southern states were all excited over John Brown's attempt to rouse the slaves to revolt. But you made a martyr of him in the North. Just his name in the song was enough to stir your men.

"From '62 to Appomattox my cousins and I served under Marse Robert. There never was such an army—Lee himself said so. You won't think this is idle boasting? Well, if it is, forgive an old man, my dear. The army of northern Virginia was the flower of the South, with regiments and divisions from all the eleven seceding states. A big proportion was young men of high culture and learning. I remember once, for a bit of fun, our company had a solemn burial for our mascot,

a tame crow. Besides speeches in English we
had a Latin oration and an ode in Greek.

"We weren't soldiers of fortune, but soldiers of duty. The men were cheerful and un-
complaining, even when things were getting
worse and worse. We weren't in the war for
any reward. Do you call it pay—eleven
dollars a month, in Confederate money? Do
you call it a fine bill of fare, the flour and
bacon and peanut coffee we had? There
were no decorations to strive for—no Victoria
Cross, no promotions given on the field for
special acts of valor. We had just the cause
of the South. We had just that one badge—
the gray uniform that gradually faded to
butternut brown. This fine gray one, Miss
Ellen, I keep for special occasions—today
and Memorial Days and reunions.

"But what made the army was our leader.
Never did soldiers have such a general, never
in all the world. The North had more men
and more money. But for a long time they
had no general so able as Lee. He was like
Washington, great in planning attacks, daring in his strategy and as daring in carrying
out his plans.

"Only think how he raised the siege of

Richmond in the Seven Days' Battles, and won at Manassas—the second battle of Bull Run you call it," the captain explained seeing the perplexed look on Ellen's face. "And what he did at Sharpsburg—I believe the North called it Antietam—and at Chancellorsville, the most brilliant of his achievements, when he used two-thirds of his men in a flank march splendidly carried out by Stonewall Jackson, and faced that great army of Hooker's with one man to five. And the three days' fighting at Gettysburg, that marked the turn of the tide.

"Funny how we happened to fight at Gettysburg, wasn't it? You see, Miss Ellen, we all needed new shoes and when we got up into southern Pennsylvania we heard there were shoes at Gettysburg. There we found the enemy and attacked before all their men could come up. No wonder the battle took three days, for the Yanks kept coming and coming, some of them from thirty-six miles away.

"In all history is there a more daring enterprise than Pickett's charge? For numbers and distance the famous Light Brigade doesn't compare with it. A full half-mile we went across that plain and up the flaming slopes of Cemetery Ridge. Oh, it was a great assault and ought to have succeeded. For the northern army had had severe losses those three days. Their morale was low. If Lee's orders had been carried out promptly and exactly and if Longstreet's divisions had supported Pickett, we'd have cut the Yanks in two and driven them from the field.

"A few years ago when the G.A.R. had a joint reunion with our U.C.V. I happened to meet two men who'd been on Cemetery Ridge that day, waiting to receive us. They told me they were out of ammunition and if the charge had been followed up, they'd have retreated in five minutes more. Why, their generals didn't know they'd won a victory and reported to Lincoln only that Lee's invasion was stopped.

"Twelve thousand of us started across. Shells hissed over us. Shot tore through us. Right and left men fell and the ranks thinned. But we pressed on, reached the foot of the hill and swarmed up it for a furious conflict with its defenders. We actually planted our flags on the crest of Cemetery Ridge. Then slowly, sullenly we rolled back across that blood-soaked plain among the heaps of dead. Gettysburg was over.

"Our shattered remnants straggled along in disorder. And there waiting for us, ready with a word of sympathy and encouragement was Marse Robert on the old gray horse Traveler that we all knew so well.

" 'Rally to your colors,' he called out. 'All this will come right in the end. We'll talk of it afterwards. Now rally!'

"He had not a word of reproach for Longstreet. He took on his own shoulders the whole responsibility, the whole blame of the defeat. But our men were not so unselfish, not so charitable. On the march south they grumbled against Longstreet and threatened to hang him. And notice this: if the Yanks thought Gettysburg a great victory they let us retreat unmolested and it was months before they attacked us again.

"Like Washington too Lee was a master in defensive warfare. He used the shield as skilfully as the sword. Look at Fredericksburg, at the long Wilderness campaign and the siege of Petersburg, the tragic retreat of that last April.

"See what he had to contend with—num-

bers against him greater than Napoleon faced
at Waterloo. With slow, steady, iron fist
Grant hammered his way onward. But he
had back of him all the men he asked for. He
had supplies without limit—food and clothes,
ammunition and muskets.

"What did Marse Robert have? A weather-
beaten army that was half shod, half fed, half
clothed. A bankrupt country that had given
all her men—her younger men and her older
men, sixteen to sixty, till President Davis
said they were using up their seedcorn and
robbing both the cradle and the grave. There
were no new recruits to throw into battle.

"The blockade was like a boa-constrictor
whose coils grew tighter and tighter. The
whole South was suffering privations and
hardships. Once Marse Robert sent a special
present to his wife—one nearly dried-up
lemon! If we fought General Grant in front
of us, we were also fighting General Want
in our rear. The other confederate states
could not help us in Virginia. Vicksburg
fell. The Mississippi was open to the sea.
Sherman marched across Georgia. The
Yanks came up into the Carolinas.

"The South was not a manufacturing

country and could not make what our armies needed. We could not sell our tobacco and cotton in Europe and then buy overseas. No, I don't think it was better generalship that won the war for the North—not Grant's iron will or Sherman's strategy. It was the blockade that did it. You won because we were exhausted.

"Often half our men, and at the end two-thirds of us were armed with sabers we took from the enemy. Was it an equal fight," he turned suddenly to Ellen, "when your men fired their Spencer rifles seven times without reloading, and we with the old Sharp's musket fired once and lowered it to put in the next cartridge? When your sappers and miners did such rapid night work after the first day at Gettysburg, while we had to throw up breastworks with our bayonets because spades were luxuries?

"Our gray uniforms were woven on plantation looms. Our cannon were mounted on farm wagons. Our swords were made at cross-road forges. So empty was the countryside that we thought ourselves well off when we found a corncrib with some grain left in it, and had parched corn to munch as we marched

along.   More than once I had to post a guard
where the artillery horses were fed, to prevent
the soldiers from taking their corn.   Yet we
kept on with unwavering courage because we
had faith in Marse Robert.

"The end came at last.   Nothing but useless loss of life could result if the struggle
was continued.   At Appomattox Lee agreed
to Grant's generous terms of surrender.
How glad we were to get those northern rations!   Go over to the desk, Randolph, and
bring me that box in the second drawer.   Yes,
that's it, the little pill-box.

"Here, Miss Ellen, is the rations our
quartermaster gave us that last morning at
Appomattox.   I saved mine as a souvenir.
Open the box and look."

Ellen took off the lid, her eyes big with
amazement.   One, two, three, four, five
grains of corn and one, two, three coffee beans.
That was a day's food for a soldier in gray.

"What a picture they made," the captain
went on, "Marse Robert in full uniform, with
sword and sash, and Grant with his boots spat-
tered all over with mud, dressed in a private's
blouse and only his shoulder-straps to show his
rank.   Lest Lee might think his careless

dress a discourtesy he took pains to explain that he'd been without his luggage for four days.

"Marse Robert came out of the McLean house and paused a moment, his eyes resting on the Virginia hills.   Then mounting on old Traveler he rode down the lane.   Somehow news of what was happening had got abroad. We were all waiting on the hillside.   When he came in sight we were up around him in an instant.   Bareheaded, with our faces wet with tears, we thronged around our general. Some of the soldiers kissed his hand.   They sobbed like children and cheered as they wept. To the very skies they shouted his name again and again.

" 'Men,' said Marse Robert, his voice quivering with emotion, 'we've fought through the war together.   I have done my best for you.   My heart is too full to say more.'

"Far over the hills our cheering was heard. The Yanks thought we were rejoicing over the surrender and the end of the war.   No, the cheers were for Marse Robert who had surrendered our muskets, but still commanded our hearts.

"Appomattox is the end of Lee's story, I

suppose, for you children in the North? A conquered chieftain, he came back to Richmond, to the house on Franklin Street."

"You remember, Ellen, where we went to the Virginia Historical Society?" put in Randolph.

"But even in defeat and failure Lee reigned in the hearts of the southern people. He was still the leader. More than he did for the South during the war, he did during the next five years. For the conflict was not over. Instead of battles there was Reconstruction. We must fight not with muskets, but with patience and self-control.

"How could Lee best serve his country? Live in peace on the beautiful estate in England which was offered him? The South needed all her sons. Accept a position in business with a big salary? But he knew nothing of life insurance. Never mind, it was enough that the company could use his name. 'But gentlemen,' he replied, 'if it is worth fifty thousand dollars a year, don't you think I ought to take good care of it? My name is not for sale.'

"In the little town of Lexington in the Shenandoah Valley he served as president of

Washington College—today we call it Washington and Lee. He was not a figurehead, but the active ruling spirit. The rest of his life he gave to train the young men of the South, sending them out prepared to help in building up her waste places.

"With the same zeal he had shown in creating an army, a nation, Lee threw himself into the task of building up a small and struggling college. What counted most was his personal influence with the students. Indeed he was creating a nation still. His own courage and patience, his forgiveness, his hope for the future, he passed on to the eager young people about him and through them to all the South, sorely in need of these things.

"Lincoln would have done much to bring the seceding states back to their early loyalty to the Union. His death left it for Lee to do. The people must be reconciled to the results of the war. They must forget their dream of a Confederacy and be cheerfully loyal to a reunited country. To set an example, he was among the first to apply for pardon from the federal government. No other man could have brought about such a prompt acceptance of the final judgment.

"A private in our camp here in Richmond told his colonel that he had taken the oath of allegiance to the United States.

" 'You've disgraced your family!'

" 'But General Lee told me to do it, sir.'

" 'Oh, that alters the case. Whatever he says is all right, I don't care what it is.'

"Against the North Marse Robert showed no trace of bitterness or resentment. In those five years there's not one word or act that his most devoted friends would wish to strike from the record though he was refused amnesty, though he was indicted for treason, though he was disenfranchised and was, till a year before his death, a man without a country.

" 'A poor old Confederate,' Lee described himself and marveled when the people received him everywhere with ovations and crowded around him to do him honor. 'Marse Robert' they called him lovingly. What other general famous in history can boast such a title?"

The captain ceased. Again his hand reached out toward the faded stars and bars. He gazed intently at the autographed picture of Lee.

Ellen looked up with eyes suspiciously bright.

"You mustn't think," she said, "that we don't honor him too. If you could only have heard the applause when Lee walked on to the stage in the play *Abraham Lincoln!* You remember how just after Appomattox a crowd of Washington people gathered in front of the White House to serenade the president and Lincoln made them a speech rejoicing that the war was over and then turned to the band and called out, 'Play Dixie! We've a right to it now!' Well, it's the same with Robert E. Lee. Here in Richmond you say Lee the Virginian. All through the South they say Lee the Confederate general. Why don't we all call him Lee the American?"

THE FEAST OF LANTERNS [1]

THE TENTH OF FEBRUARY

Very, very early this morning Wang Tzu and her sister wakened. Noiselessly they slipped out of the women's quarters with their mother. Dawn had not yet touched the sky with rose and gold. Tzu shivered as they hurried to the temple to pray.

When the old sundial warned them that eight o'clock was near they flitted back from prayers to rice. For after that hour the men would seek the gods with gifts of lotus flowers.

Today Wang Tzu is wearing her best robe of violet satin embroidered with lemon chrysanthemums. It is slashed open above a vest and trousers of delicate green tied with silver cords, each ending in a pearl.

[1] The "Feast of Lanterns" is a movable holiday like our Easter or the Jewish new year. Books of travel vary greatly in giving its date, but it is always in February. It is the fifteenth of the first month of the old Chinese calendar.

She glances up at her mother. How she sways on her tiny feet, like a lily in the wind! How lovely her new robe is—brocade of jade green with dark blue flower-shaped embroidery, over trousers of orange silk!

Over the whole house, over all the courtyards where live Tzu's uncles and cousins there is today a hum of merriment. Every one is glad and gay. For of all the many holidays in China, this is the one most loved, the day when the spirits of the dead return.

"Remember," says the grandmother, "they are here threading their kindly, silent way through the crowd. They are watching and enjoying everything."

In the grass and in the garden paths bundles of joss sticks are burning. Little hills of white ash heap up as the children slip in fresh bundles before the first ones go out. Incense burns for the honored guests, for no unpleasant smell must offend their nostrils. For them the fire-crackers crackle out in great bursts and the drums beat and rattle to scare away the devils, lest they injure or annoy the Wang ancestors.

For days and weeks Tzu's grandmother has been preparing for this festival. She sent the servants to the lantern shops. Lanterns shaped like animals, like men, like ships they chose, such fragile things.

"The place was so crowded," Sun Moy described it to the two girls, "it was hard to get out without crushing my purchases. So I hoisted them on a bamboo pole and squeezed my way through. Time after time I did so, for I bought more than two hundred. A splendid feast we shall have this year!"

For days too the kitchens have buzzed as the cooks made sweetmeats for this holiday. There are flat, round, crisp mooncakes sweetened with honey.

"Mountains of them!" is Tzu's description when she stops trying to count them. "They're heaped up in thousands on grandmother's lacquer trays. I can't miss the first batch that Mother gave to the greedy kitchen gods licking their fat lips so hungrily: that was to make sure that the rest will not be tough."

With the mooncakes were made the small balls of mincemeat covered with sugar. As round as a billiard ball they are and about two-thirds as large. A perfect, snowy white they must be, and made with the greatest care, for they are a part of the ceremony. And when the feast day comes every household eats them in unbelievable quantities.

Yesterday every one—mothers and children and servants—helped string the lanterns like garlands from tree to tree. Criss-cross they go in every courtyard, till Tzu declares her grandmother owns miles of lanterns. There are all the new ones Sun Moy brought from the city shops. There are some that are heirlooms.

"Why do you keep them put away with your jades and bronze, Grandmother?" Tzu asked as one after another the delicate things of gauze and jewels were brought out.

"Why not?" was the answer. "They are almost as valuable."

Inside a Chinese house one thing of beauty never jostles against another. One flower in a fine vase and the room is adorned. But outside for this feast of lanterns there is the most lavish decoration. Every tree, every shrub, every bridge, every point from which something can hang is trimmed with streamers, with artificial flowers, with strings of gilt, with festoons of lanterns. The whole place throbs with color, for the Chinese love bright hues and have wonderful skill in combining them.

Wherever she looks Tzu's eyes see lanterns. They decorate a carved stone seat. They trim a pretty balcony. They hang from the fantastic railing of a garden bridge. Lanterns, lanterns everywhere!

Only one spot is without them—the silkworm houses. The light and the heat of the candles might creep in and harm the delicate worms. Instead the houses are trimmed with rich scented flowers, for silkworms love sweet fragrance and are nourished by it. And at night the fireflies will hang their jeweled lights about the thatched houses and make a break in the wilderness of lamps.

The whole day is one long holiday packed with pleasure. There are sports to watch— juggling and wrestling. There are a pageant and a play. given by actors from a city theater. And all the time children and grownups alike munch their mincemeat balls.

For the little folks there are gay balloons. Some are tied to the glass bracelets on their wrists. Some are held by strings in little yellow hands. Some Ting and Tzu set free. From these balls filled with gas hang delicate little chimes of bells whose soft music tinkles down between the crackling of the fireworks.

But now twilight is coming. The great throbbing hour of all the festival is at hand—the procession of lanterns. Tzu looks up at the sky, a velvet blue powdered with brilliant stars. She watches the servants lighting all the lanterns in the courtyard. "Criss-cross, criss-cross for miles!" she repeats to herself. From every bough of every tree in the garden lanterns hang that the spirits moving about their old homes may have light to see.

It is time for the procession to start.

"How gaily dressed the bearers are!" Tzu says to her grandmother. "But why are their faces all so serious and grave?"

"It is a solemn festival, child. They know the meaning of their task. But hush now, they are coming into sight."

From the great gates at the entrance of the estate the procession of lanterns slowly approaches. First is a group of little boys each carrying two swaying, gauzy lamps filled with the incense of burning sandalwood. Then a long line of older boys. In twos, in threes, in wide ranks they come. Here one walks alone to show the beauty of some rare lantern.

How beautiful they are! How odd! No

two alike! In all of China no flower grows
that is not shown here. Every fruit is pictured, every jewel cut into some exquisite
shape. Some lanterns are painted, some are
wonderfully embroidered. It takes an artist
a year to decorate one of them. For all their
fragile surface some are so heavy that they are
slung on stout bamboo poles resting on the
shoulders of two men.

Who could describe all the lanterns in this
procession to honor the spirits of the dead?
There are birds and gilded fish, beasts from
the jungle, tame farm animals. There are
squirrels and cranes, ducks and eagles and pea-
cocks. There are orange buds and flowers,
wistaria and cacti, clusters of grapes and snow-
capped mountains in red eruption. There are
warships and barges of state. There are tem-
ples and gods and dancing girls and mandarins
and babies in their tall cradles. And every
lantern is brilliant with rich colors.

"Oh, oh! See that lovely tulip!" cries out
Tzu.

"And the chrysanthemum just behind it!"
exclaims her sister.

"There comes the larkspur—blue and rose.
And the little humming birds!"

Most of the time the children watch quietly, breathlessly. But when Tzu sees a marvelous lantern shifting to another shape at a slight touch of wind she whispers to her grandmother, "Look, look! How is it made—that rose changing to a rose-pink gull? What skill it must take!"

Before her very eyes the red tulip changes to a cluster of cherries dangling just out of reach. The gentian becomes a bird in flight. The kittens play with a ball.

Such marvels of lanterns! Some roll along on the ground and yet keep lighted. Some gallop like a horse. Some whirl like a top. There are ships that sail. There are soldiers that march.

In silence the children and the grownups look on. When some lantern of special beauty passes they give a great sigh of pleasure. For all the noise of fire-crackers and drums, it has been a day of solemn courtesy to welcome the homecoming of the dead.

For more than two thousand years this feast of lanterns has been celebrated in China. When the moon was at the first full round of the year the devout Chinese used to pray and sacrifice—a formal rite of worship in the temple.   After eight hundred years the lanterns were added.   Gradually the day changed from a strict religious beginning to this home festival.

Suddenly the silence is broken.   Among the children there is a happy whispering.

"The dragon!   The dragon is coming!"

Dragons have already passed, to be sure, along with waxen lilies and scarlet trumpet flowers.   But this is the GREAT DRAGON.   To announce its approach boys let loose hundreds of balloons coated with phosphorus.   The darkness of the night is radiant with light.

Forty, fifty, sometimes a hundred men carry the dragon.   They are clad in gray to show as little as possible.   The splendid, terrible monster seems to move along without their help.   He's a gorgeous beast, horned and scaly, with painted sides.

Every few minutes he turns his awful head. He opens wide his terrible jaws and breathes out a soft mist of perfume.   And with the rain of scent shower down the writhing monster's gifts—sweetmeats and little mascots made of twisted jade, that bring good luck to the recipient.

Slowly the dragon passes on its long, fiery

way. Then comes a band of little girls singing a goodnight hymn. The feast of lanterns is ended.

"Ah, it's over," Tzu says to herself half sighing. "This is the end of our three weeks of holidays. Tomorrow lessons begin again —school seven days a week till next New Year's. But the feast of lanterns—each time this beauty-keeping festival is richer and lovelier than before. It's our offering to the spirit of our ancestors. It is the very soul of China!"

THE LAWYER FROM THE
MIDDLE WEST

THE TWELFTH OF FEBRUARY

"How did you happen to come to America?"

"Ah," is the eager reply from Italian or Pole or Russian, "I heard of your Lincoln. So I come to his country."

"What biography is most asked for by your boys and girls?"

"Lincoln's," promptly says the librarian in the children's room. "That shelf is always empty. One lad recommends his life to another with the comment, 'This is a great book! Why, he was one of us—a great man, but like us!'"

In the history of notable men the world over there's nothing to equal the growth of Abraham Lincoln's fame. But in February of 1809 who would have guessed that the baby in that one-roomed log cabin in Kentucky would have his birthday celebrated everywhere? Who would have foretold greatness and fame for a boy whose father could not read or write, who was poor and shiftless, restlessly moving from one place to another and dropping a little lower with each move?

Who would have said there was much of a future for a lad who for nine years went to school whenever there was a school to go to, but not twelve months in all? Yet at seventeen Abraham Lincoln had learned to read and to read well, to write a clear hand, and to solve problems in arithmetic not going beyond the "rule of three." With this meager foundation he kept on studying and pulled himself out of ignorance, as he put it, by his own bootstraps.

In that household pinched by poverty candles were a great luxury. By the flickering glow of the fire the boy worked his sums using a wooden shovel for a slate and a bit of charcoal for pencil. When the shovel was covered with figures he shaved it off and began again.

Lying on the floor with a blazing pine knot for his light he read eagerly, hungrily. The six books he owned he devoured over and over and over—Æsop's *Fables, Pilgrim's Progress, Robinson Crusoe,* Plutarch's *Lives,* Euclid and the Bible. He read all the books he could beg or borrow, no matter if securing one meant a walk of twenty miles and back. He read at night after long hours of work. He read every spare minute during the busy day, while he walked down the road, while he rested his horses at the end of a long furrow.

"What are you reading, Abe?" a farmer asked the lanky boy cocked up on a haystack with a book.

"I'm not reading, I'm studying."

"Well then, what are you studying?"

"Law."

"He spoke as proud as Cicero," the farmer described years afterward.

From the time he was a small boy he worked and worked hard. He helped his father clear the forest, plow the ground, plant and harvest corn. For the neighbors he did all sorts of odd jobs. Pioneers began to say that he was above the average backwoods lad. He was gentle and tender and loving. Would the ordinary ten-year-old child, some months after the death of his mother, have written to a minister begging him to come one hundred miles and conduct the delayed funeral service at her grave?

Would an ordinary boy have borrowed Farmer Crawford's copy of Weems' *Life of Washington* and been so thrilled by its story of heroism and sacrifice and love of country that he slept with it under his pillow, to start reading the moment he awoke? Would the ordinary lad, when a storm came up and driving rain blew in through the chinks in the logs and soaked pillow and boy's head and the precious book as well, have gone sadly to the owner and asked how he could pay for it?

"Three days' corn shucking," said Crawford.

The boy was honest. He was shrewd too.

"Will that pay for the book or only for the damage?"

"Well, it's not much account now to me or anybody else. You pull fodder three days and the book is yours."

What promise of greatness was there in any of the careers tried by this young man in homespun clothes? He did whatever work was offered in the neighborhood—splitting fence rails, making shelves and chairs, minding the baby. He clerked in a store and won the nickname "Honest Abe," because he walked two miles to give a woman six cents more in change. He was elected captain of a company of volunteers in a war with the Black Hawk Indians. No hint here that he would one day be commander-in-chief of army and navy. He was surveyor and postmaster in New Salem. He owned half of a store that failed, his partner died, and left Lincoln to meet the debts—the "national debt" he used to call that twelve hundred dollars, and paid the last cent of it after seventeen years of struggle and saving.

Twice he took a cargo down the Mississippi on a flatboat. He saw slaves toiling on the plantations and on the river wharves. He saw them herded like cattle, torn from their families and their homes, chained and sold at auction. The scenes in the slave market at New Orleans made him sick at heart. As they turned to go Lincoln said to his friends with an earnestness that they remembered, "If I ever get a chance to strike a blow at slavery, I'll hit it hard!" What opportunity would come to him? No suggestion here that he would one day free four million slaves.

Between times he read what law books he could get. In 1836 he was admitted to the bar and the next year moved to Springfield, the capital of the state. Riding into town on a borrowed horse, with all his worldly possessions packed into his saddle-bags he set up as a lawyer. Men said, "He'll never make a good lawyer—he's too honest."

From one town to another he rode the circuit. He began to win cases because he thought things through to the end, because he was logical and could make others see his reasoning, because he was absolutely fair. A wonderful knack he had of winning men over to his opinion. Slowly but surely he forged to the front in his profession.

"Where did that long-armed creature come from," asked Stanton when he and Lincoln met in a Cincinnati court in 1855, "and what can he expect to do in this case?"

A long-legged, long-armed country lawyer, why celebrate his birthday?

For years the question of slavery had been the most important matter before the nation. It was definitely settled by Congress in 1820, then again in 1850. But it would not stay settled. Again and again it pushed its way into public affairs. During his one term in Congress Lincoln voted forty times or more for the Wilmot Proviso and other bills touch-

ing on the question of slavery in the territory
taken from Mexico.

In 1854 came Stephen A. Douglas, the
"little giant," with a new scheme. Let the
people of each state decide for themselves
whether they would have slavery or no. At
the passage of this bill a storm of indignation
rose in the North. Back home again in Illinois Douglas made a speech defending the
new law. All eyes turned to Lincoln to answer it.

He had definitely given up active interest
in politics. He was not a candidate for a second term in Congress. He had settled down
to work hard at the practise of law. Now
thoroughly roused he threw himself into the
struggle. He replied to Douglas in a speech
where his clear reasoning swept his listeners
along. Here was a leader for the men opposed to the Kansas-Nebraska bill.

A new political party came into being.
Among themselves the Republicans disagreed
on nearly every question. They thought alike
on just one thing. They were against the
spread of slavery. For the first election, that
of 1856, they had little time to organize and
lost the day.

Two years later a senator was to be chosen in Illinois. Douglas wanted to be reëlected. The Republicans of the state fixed on Lincoln to run against him. All Illinois listened to the seven debates where these two men spoke from the same platform. All the North was listening to this new leader who showed a grasp of national affairs.

"Lincoln's a dangerous man," said a life-long Democrat. "He makes you believe what he says in spite of yourself!"

He was an orator whose simple reasoning they could follow. He pressed the brilliant Douglas with plain, blunt questions and demanded plain answers. He stood for what he knew to be right and said to his friends, anxiously urging him not to make the house-divided-against-itself speech, "But it is true. I'd rather be defeated with that speech than win without it."

Southerners too were listening. In this country lawyer from the middle west, the "big giant," they sensed a distant threat to slavery. They stored up the answers Douglas made to his plain questions, answers that offended the South and made the "little giant" unpopular. Some of these questions Lincoln's friends begged him not to ask. Douglas would answer them in such a way that even men opposed to slavery would vote for him and that would make him senator.

"Yes," was the reply, "but I'm after larger game. If Douglas so answers he can never be president. 1860 is worth a hundred of this!"

He was right. Douglas won the senatorship. But the debates made Lincoln known. Men were curious to see and hear for themselves this obscure man from Illinois. He was invited to speak in several eastern cities. At Cooper Union in New York, before the leaders of the new party, he made an address that was famous indeed.

"When Lincoln rose to speak," says a man who was there that February night, "I was greatly disappointed. He was tall—oh, how tall!—and so angular and awkward that I had for an instant a feeling of pity for so ungainly a man. His clothes were black and ill-fitting, badly wrinkled—as if they had been jammed carelessly into a large trunk. His bushy head, with the stiff black hair thrown back, was balanced on a long and lean head-stalk; and when he raised his hands in an opening gesture, I noticed that they were very large.

"He began in a low tone of voice, as if he were used to speaking outdoors and was afraid of speaking too loud. I said to myself, 'Old fellow, you won't do. It's all very well for the wild west, but this will never go down in New York.' But pretty soon he began to get into his subject; he straightened up, made regular and graceful gestures; his face lighted as with an inward fire—the whole man was transfigured. I forgot his clothes, his personal appearance. Presently forgetting myself, I was on my feet with the rest, yelling like a wild Indian, cheering this wonderful man.

"In the close parts of his argument you could hear the gentle sizzling of the gas burners. When he reached a climax the thunders of applause were terrific. When I came out of the hall, my face glowing with excitement and my frame all aquiver, a friend with his eyes aglow asked me what I thought of Abe Lincoln, the rail-splitter? I said, 'He's the greatest man since St. Paul!' And I think so still."

This Cooper Union speech was published in the papers. It was printed and sent broadcast as a pamphlet. It was like a bugle-call for the election of 1860. It gave a leader to the Republicans not of his home state, but of the nation.

Over all the other candidates Lincoln was

nominated for the presidency. As he had prophesied the answers to his questions made it impossible for the South to vote for Douglas. The Democratic party split and had two tickets. After an exciting campaign Abraham Lincoln was elected by the largest popular vote ever given up to that time for any president. Some men had begun to call him great. But the United States has had many presidents whose birthdays pass with no celebration.

That was a critical time in our history. The southern states were threatening to leave the Union, to secede and form a government based on slavery. Let them go, let them go in peace, urged many in the North. Keep them in the Union, argued conservative business men, give in to them on some points, but keep them. All those trying months between election and inauguration Lincoln could do nothing.

Indeed after he became president he must still wait in patience. If there was to be war he did not wish to strike the first blow. By the fourth of March of 1861 seven states had seceded and formed the Confederate States of America. Four others joined them. Their

Congress passed a bill organizing an army. Still Lincoln waited.

On the twelfth of April the Confederates bombarded Fort Sumter in the harbor of Charleston and war began. Now that the seceding states had fired the first shot Lincoln lost not a moment. He called for seventy-five thousand men. More than five million volunteered. The patriotism of the North caught fire. The people had been vacillating and unsettled. Now they took up Lincoln's cry, "The Union! The Union!"

The South had at the start many advantages. The sympathy of foreign countries was theirs. They had been making ready for war. They had great supplies of ammunition. They had trained officers to call on. Their one chance was to win quickly.

If the war was protracted the North had reserves of strength that must in the long run bring victory. Twenty-two million people against nine, and of these more than a third were slaves. Only a patient man could await the outcome of such a struggle. But Lincoln was patient.

Infinite patience he had with his cabinet,

men who had run against him for the nomination, now his advisers through four years of crisis. Able men they were, but varying widely in their views.

"You can never drive such a team," warned the president's old friends.

Nobody but a Lincoln could have kept cordial relations with Seward, the scholarly secretary of state, a man of notable ancestry and fine presence, who had a notion he could control a backwoods president and keep him straight, who offered to outline a government policy, who even prepared an inaugural address. Who else could have managed Stanton who had declared he'd make a president of Lincoln, but in the end was himself made a good secretary of war? Only a master of men could have shut his eyes to all personal issues among his cabinet members and held them to the great task before them—of saving the Union.

From the very first Lincoln saw that though the war had been caused by slavery, its suppression was not the primary purpose of the conflict. It became suddenly a secondary issue and fell into the background. First in importance was the preservation of the Union.

"My course," said Lincoln to members of a peace congress, "is as plain as a turnpike road. It is marked out by the constitution. I am in no doubt which way to go."

Lincoln was patient too with his generals. Untrained in the art of war he was, some people said, a better commander than any in the federal army. Day and night he studied the campaigns in the east and middle west. On a large wall map he followed every step of the northern troops. He pored over military books. Often he spent the night by the telegraph in the war office, intent on the last dispatches from the front. So practical was his knowledge that he often surprised his officers by his directions and suggestions.

In 1861 Lincoln had no great general, no one to offset Lee. It was the war itself that made them. Six different men he tried in command of the army of the Potomac, the pride and hope of the North. Five of them were misfits. The first adopted a do-nothing policy when the people demanded "On to Richmond!" He wore away his own reputation and the patience of president and country by his endless delays, his marching and countermarching, his requests for more men, more horses, more munitions, more everything.

"If General McClellan has no use for the army of the Potomac, I'd like to borrow it for a little while," said Lincoln.

In the end the president found his man, a quiet man from his own state, a man who could go ahead with cool persistency of purpose, with the grip of a bulldog. Grant had enemies who urged Lincoln to remove him.

"But I need this man," was the reply. "He fights."

"Oh, Mr. Lincoln, he drinks."

"Do you know what brand of whiskey? I'd like to send a barrel of it to each of my other generals."

With all the help of an able cabinet, with the loyal support of the North, with generals and soldiers who could fight and win, or lose and fight again, the burden of the four years of war rested on Abraham Lincoln. His was the final responsibility for success or failure. Each new crisis he met with the same unflinching courage, the same patience, the same gentleness.

Week by week, month by month his grave face took on a new and deeper sadness. It was thin and drawn. The dark gray eyes were heavy and sunken. All the light had gone out of them. Slower grew his step, more bent his shoulders. In every line of his great body there was utter weariness. His work was never finished. The burden and the worry were always with him.

The only relief he found was in his fund of stories. Once at a cabinet meeting he read aloud a passage from a humorous book. His listeners were amazed, then disgusted. Not one of them smiled.

"Gentlemen," he asked with a sigh, "why don't you laugh? With the fearful strain that is upon me night and day, if I did not laugh I should die. You need this medicine as much as I do."

The two outstanding events of the war were Lee's invasions of the North: the battle of Antietam followed by Lincoln's emancipation proclamation giving freedom to the slaves; and the battle at Gettysburg followed by the promotion of Grant who replied, when asked how he proposed to win, "By pegging away and wearing them down."

Many enemies Lincoln had. They criticised his management of the war. They urged him to free the slaves immediately.

They condemned his every act. Opposition he had aplenty—from quarrelsome members of the cabinet, from an endless procession of office seekers and callers, from the press with comments that were frequently hostile and bitter.

Another presidential election occurred in 1864. There was a loud demand for Lincoln's withdrawal from office. From all sides his enemies attacked him. Some newspapers tried to prove him unfit for the presidency. Shortly before the election Grant's troops suffered fearful losses in Virginia. Against the advice of his friends Lincoln took the unpopular step of drafting half a million more men.

But the people, the common people who make up the backbone of the nation, had come to know him and to love him. They laughed at his eccentricities and despite them idolized him. In their homes and around the camp fires they told his stories. They were impressed by his comparison of the North to the old Dutchman who refused to swap horses in the middle of the stream. This man so firm, so modest, so tender, so full of quaint stories and homely midwestern phrases, this man was one of them. "Father Abraham" they called him, the father of a new nation reborn from the bloodshed and suffering of civil war.

By a vast majority he was reëlected in November. "This," telegraphed Grant, "is worth more to the country than a battle won."

Finally the tide turned. The beginning of the end came into sight. In a fairly steady stream the North began to receive news of successes. One by one Lincoln's four plans had been carried through: to win over the border states and thus prevent the spread of the rebellion; to open the Mississippi cutting the South in two; to blockade the southern ports so that no cotton could be shipped to Europe, no purchases made there be brought into the country; and last but not least, the plan that took the longest to carry through and cost the most in lives and money, to capture Richmond.

"We've had a hard time of it, Mary," the president said to his wife as they drove out that balmy April afternoon when the air was filled with the scent of lilacs, "since we came to Washington. But the war is over and with God's blessing we may hope for four years of peace and happiness and then we'll go back to Illinois and pass the rest of our lives in quiet."

Dedicate ourselves to the great task remaining before us, he had said on the battlefield of Gettysburg. In his second inaugural address he described that task: "With malice toward none, with charity for all, with firmness in the right as God gives us to see the right, let us bind up the nation's wounds."

But Lincoln was not to be the leader of the people in the second part of this work. A few hours after that drive with his wife he was struck down by the bullet of an actor who pushed into his box at the theater. All night he lay unconscious and died the next morning. His life unfinished? Through fearful storms he had brought the ship of state safely into port and dropped anchor.

A great loss to the North, a loss to the world, most of all an irreparable loss to the South who had no better friend than this country lawyer from the middle west.

In one bright flash the people saw how great a man had fallen. Instead of waving flags and cheers of victory they had only tears and sorrow. As the funeral train draped in black passed on its long journey to his old home in Springfield, men and women stood silent with bared heads to do him honor. Kings and emperors paid their tributes. Soldiers and workingmen, children and ex-slaves sent their pennies to build a monument to Lincoln.

By whatever standard men measure he is one of the greatest—this American born in a log cabin, whose life stood for human freedom, for greater justice, more good will and love among mankind. Since 1865 all the world has been raising memorials in his honor. Many a town in Italy, many a village in distant Poland has a street called after him.

Statesmen and patriots study his life that they may the better serve their country. Men and women resolve to imitate his beautiful charity, his public spirit. Children learn his story, inspired to a like effort, no matter what their environment. The shelf in the public library where the Lincoln books belong is always empty.

As Sam says to Enrico, "He's a great man. But he's just one of us."

THE GOOD SAINT VALENTINE

In the city of Rome there once lived an emperor named Claudius. He is known in history as Claudius the Cruel.

Near his palace was a beautiful temple where served the priest Valentine. Dearly the Romans loved him. They thronged into the temple to hear his words. Before the fire that burned always on the altar they knelt to ask his blessing. Rich and poor, wise and ignorant, old and young, patricians and common people flocked to Valentine.

In the Roman empire wars broke out. Claudius summoned the citizens forth to battle. Year after year the fighting continued. Many of the Romans were loath to go. The married men did not want to leave their families. The younger men did not wish to leave their sweethearts. The emperor was angry when soldiers were too few. He ordered that no more marriages should be celebrated, that all engagements must be broken off immediately.

Many a young Roman went off to the wars in sorrow, leaving his love. Many a Roman maiden died of grief as a result of this decree.

Now the good priest Valentine heard of the emperor's command and was very sad. When a young couple came to the temple, secretly he united them in marriage in front of the sacred altar. Another pair sought his aid. In secret he wedded them. Others came and quietly were married. Valentine was the friend of lovers in every district of Rome.

But such secrets could not be kept for long. At last word of Valentine's acts reached the palace. Claudius the Cruel was angry, exceedingly angry. He summoned his soldiers.

"Go! Take that priest in the temple! Cast him into a dungeon! No man in Rome, priest or no, shall disobey my commands!"

Valentine was dragged from the temple, dragged away from the altar where stood a young maiden and a Roman youth, ready to wed. Off to prison the soldiers took him.

His friends, and the good priest had many,

many friends, interceded with Claudius. In
vain. Well was he named Claudius the Cruel.
In a dungeon Valentine languished and died.
His devoted friends buried him in the church
of St. Praxedes. When you go to Rome you
can see the very place. It was the year 270,
on the fourteenth of February.

Another story says that Valentine was one
of the early Christians in those far-away days
when that meant danger and death. For
helping some Christian martyrs he was seized,
dragged before the prefect of Rome and cast
into jail. There he cured the keeper's daughter of blindness. When the cruel emperor
learned of this miracle he gave orders that
Valentine should be beheaded.

Long years before 270, when Rome was first
founded it was surrounded by a wilderness.
Great hordes of wolves roamed over the countryside. Among their many gods the Romans
had one named Lupercus who watched over
the shepherds and their flocks. In his honor
they held a great feast in February of each
year and called it the Lupercalia.

Even after the wilderness had been cleared
away and there was no longer such danger

from the wolves, the people kept this feast day. One of the amusements at the Lupercalia was a lottery where the names of Roman maidens were placed in a box and drawn out by the young men. The girl whose name he drew each man accepted as his love—for a year or longer.

After Christianity was firmly established the priests wanted the people to forget the old heathen gods. But they did not wish to do away with all their feasts and sports. So they kept the Lupercalia and called it Valentine's day.

Into the lottery they put the names not of maidens, but of different saints. The name drawn out by each young man was called his valentine. Throughout the year he must imitate the holy life of his saint.

During the medieval days of chivalry names of English maidens and bachelors were put into the box and drawn out in pairs. Each couple exchanged presents. The girl became the man's valentine for that year. On his sleeve he wore her name. It was his bounden duty to attend and protect her.

This old, old custom of drawing names on the fourteenth of February was considered a

good omen in love affairs. Often it foretold
a wedding. For since the beginning of things
this has been lovers' day, a time for love making, for giving and receiving love tokens.

So far as history tells us the first modern
valentines date from the early years of the fifteenth century. The young French duke of
Orleans, captured at the battle of Agincourt,
was kept a prisoner in the Tower of London
for many years. To his wife he wrote poem
after poem, real valentines. About sixty of
them remain. You may see some among the
royal papers in the British Museum.

Flowers as valentines are nearly two hundred years later. A daughter of Henry IV
of France gave a party in honor of St. Valentine. Each lady received a beautiful bouquet
of flowers from the man chosen as her valentine.

Thus from Italy and France and England
has come the pretty custom of sending our
friends loving messages on this day. With
flowers, with heart-shaped candies, with lacy
valentines whose frills and furbelows hide the
initials of the sender we honor the good priest
who disobeyed Claudius the Cruel.

THE MASTER OF "MOUNT VERNON"

THE TWENTY-SECOND OF FEBRUARY

"Forward, march!"

"Halt! Present—"

"Time to come in, boys," called Mr. Hobby, the school master. "A real general little George Washington is," he said to himself as the child put away his wooden sword and British flag. "Well, his great-grandfather was colonel in the Virginia militia. I guess he comes naturally by leadership."

Captain and general the boy was in marches across the school yard, in parades and bloodless battles. English soldiers fighting French and Indians, his little army won victory after victory. He was still the leader when there were other games than war.

"Let's ask George to settle it," the boys would say when a dispute arose. "He's always generous and just and fair."

During his boyhood on the Virginia plantation there was constant talk of battles. A third war between France and England had begun. On the frontiers was the never-ending fight with the red men. Lawrence Washington, George's half-brother, had been a soldier. From him and his friends, officers in the British navy and in the militia of Virginia, the boy heard many a tale of adventure on land and sea. Eagerly he listened to their stories of the French wars, and heard them prophesy more fighting with their old enemy to win the Ohio country, as they called the land just over the mountains.

"I like George's high spirit and honor. He's a fine lad," said Lawrence Washington and after their father's death took him under his care. Through his friends in the navy he obtained for his young brother a warrant as midshipman. But Mrs. Washington would not give her consent, though the story is that his luggage had already been sent aboard a man-of-war anchored in the Potomac.

"No, my son, you are too young. The navy offers many dangers and temptations. What future does it give a middy?"

Much of Washington's training was due to his mother. Love of order, power to govern he learned from her. Strictly and sensibly she brought up her children. She demanded prompt obedience. On courage and manliness and honor she laid great stress. Is there a better foundation on which to build character?

In his last year of school he studied surveying. This knowledge helped him later in his work on the plantation, in charting camps and forts, in choosing the site for a new capital city. The work of surveying land in that new country would give him plenty of occupation and bring him in money.

In March of 1748 Washington changed suddenly from a sixteen-year-old schoolboy to a man ready for his first important work in the world. There was a full month of hard and rough frontier living while he surveyed the Fairfax estates. Through forests and over mountains he and his companions carried their instruments, crossing icy streams, shooting wild turkeys for their food, sleeping in tent or cabin or under the stars.

"Do your work thoroughly," his mother had said over and over till it was impressed upon him.

The reports of this wilderness trip, with

maps and figures showing clearly the Fairfax properties, so pleased the owner that he helped his young friend secure a license as public surveyor. Till he was twenty Washington continued in that work, often away from home for weeks at a time. He built a reputation as a skilled woodsman and an accurate surveyor. His figures became part of the county records and are still used in Virginia.

Lawrence Washington was ill and resigned his command in the colonial army. For his brother he secured the post of military inspector with the rank of major. A few months later he died leaving to George the guardianship of his daughter and "Mount Vernon," his great plantation on the Potomac. Giving up surveying the young man took up these new responsibilities. Already he had shown that he could be depended on in an emergency.

The emergency was not long in coming in Virginia.

On the frontier affairs grew threatening. The English kings had granted lands in America reaching indefinitely westward from the Atlantic. Now the French working their way down from their settlements in Canada and

planning to unite them with New Orleans by
a chain of forts, were entering the Ohio country. Both nations realized how valuable this
section would one day be—valuable for colonies, for trade with the Indians.

Rumors came that the French were building a fort on the Ohio river and persuading the
red men to help them against the English.
The governor of Virginia determined to demand an explanation from the invaders.

"I must learn exactly where the fort is and
how strongly it's defended," he said. "So my
messenger must be a trained soldier to report
all that he sees. He must be able to make
friends with the Indians. He must be a good
woodsman, able to travel through the forests
at this time of year, for winter's just beginning. Where can I find such a man?"

Some one suggested Major Washington.

"Just the one! I'll send him at once."

The very day the young man received his
orders he began making preparations—engag-
ing guides, collecting a supply of horses and
provisions, of guns and ammunition. The
journey was seven hundred and fifty miles
through almost unbroken wilderness. The
letter to the French commander at Fort Du-

quesne was delivered and an answer received.

The return trip was still more difficult. There was deep snow. The pack horses gave out. With knapsack and gun Washington set off on foot, was led astray by his Indian guide, was jerked overboard into freezing water when crossing a swift stream on a raft; but pressing steadily forward in the face of the worst possible weather he brought the Frenchman's reply to the governor.

In the Ohio country the young major had kept both eyes and ears open. He wrote such a good account of his journey with such detailed information about the fort and its garrison, the surrounding country and the Indians that it was published as a government record.

The French defied the English and refused to withdraw. This meant war, war carried on by the colonies alone for a year, then taken up by the mother country. Veteran soldiers were sent over from England. General Braddock was appointed to take Fort Duquesne. Now this dashing Irish officer was an experienced commander, but knew nothing of the Ohio country. For the Virginia troops he felt only contempt.

With an absurd amount of baggage for those forest roads, Braddock set out. Without sending any skirmishers ahead he crossed the river some eight miles from the fort, though he had been warned of the danger of ambuscades. In their brilliant scarlet uniforms, their arms glittering, flags flying, drums gaily beating, his troops swept forward. The straggling Virginians in their hunting costumes made a sorry showing in comparison.

With admiring eyes Washington who was serving on Braddock's staff, looked on as the British swung across a wide clearing fringed with wooded hills. Suddenly there was a loud cry. The crack of a rifle followed. From the forest on the heights came a storm of bullets. Into the deadliest sort of ambush they had marched.

At the first volley the colonials spread out, each man for himself, taking cover behind trees in Indian fashion.

"Shelter your men in the same way," suggested Washington.

"No, hiding behind trees is like cowardice in the face of the enemy," was the proud answer.

The panic-stricken men were reformed into

shoulder-to-shoulder ranks.   They were a perfect target for the concealed foe.   By the score they were shot down.   Disciplined veterans of England, they streamed away in headlong flight.   Braddock fell sorely wounded. Washington took over the command and organized the retreat.   Only his courage and coolness saved the army from utter destruction.

A month later he was given command of all the forces of Virginia.   The next years were full of vexatious, often thankless work.   The long frontier must be defended from Indian attacks.   Money was lacking.   His soldiers were raw material.   Sometimes the colony's officials neglected this branch of the service.

During these months Washington learned the truth of the old saying, "It's a poor workman who constantly finds fault with his tools." He formed the habit of making one thing serve when he couldn't get another.   He entered this war with the French a daring young officer.   He came out of it a well-disciplined commander.   Much he had learned from the British.   He knew that they were not invincible.

In 1758 Washington met Martha Custis, a

guest at a friend's house where he stopped to dine. At first sight they fell in love. The wedding was a brilliant scene, for this young colonel was a person of importance in Virginia. The governor was there in his gold and scarlet costume. There were English and colonial officers in dress uniforms. There were ladies in picturesque draped gowns. The bride wore white silk shot with threads of silver. The groom was in a blue suit trimmed with scarlet.

They lived in Williamsburg, the capital of the colony, that Washington might attend the meetings of the House of Burgesses to which he was elected during his last campaign. As soon as these official duties permitted they moved to "Mount Vernon."

Life there was not a time of luxury and idleness. Washington studied the best methods of raising crops. He planned new buildings and kept the farm accounts. He made tools and looked after the welfare of his slaves. He was ambitious to make his the model plantation of Virginia. Such was his reputation for honesty and fairness that barrels of flour marked "George Washington—Mount Vernon" were passed without inspection at foreign ports and brought the highest prices. He found time to hunt with his old friends, to fish and shoot, to attend dinners and dances in the neighborhood, to be host to countless persons. Seldom did he miss a meeting of the Burgesses. He took the keenest interest in public questions.

The matter most discussed was no longer a contest with the French, but England's treatment of her colonies. Washington was in the House when a new member, a young lawyer named Patrick Henry, made a bold speech warning the king not to tax America without her consent, even if the money was to be used for the debts of the late war. Against the stamp act there was such fierce opposition that the British abandoned it. For a while it seemed as if there would be no further difficulty.

Then trouble broke out anew. Massachusetts was interfered with—a military governor, soldiers quartered upon the people, the Boston massacre came in quick succession. More and more serious grew the quarrel between colonies and mother country. Clouds of war were gathering. Washington was slow in making up his mind which side to take; but once he decided there was no shadow of turning.

A congress representing all the colonies was summoned to meet in Philadelphia. As one of her seven delegates Virginia sent Washington. He had seldom spoken in the House of Burgesses. Now he made one eloquent speech:

"I will raise a thousand men, enlist them at my own expense, and march myself at their head for the relief of Boston."

But that Congress of 1774 contented itself with sending a petition to the king explaining the difficulty and demanding fair treatment.

Neither king 'nor Parliament paid any attention to the petition. Reluctantly the colonies prepared for war. Washington was chosen to go to a second Continental Congress and showed his opinions by wearing to Philadelphia the old blue and red uniform which he had had when commanding the forces of Virginia. Martha Washington stood on the steps of "Mount Vernon" and watched him ride away with Henry and Randolph.

"I hope you'll all stand firm," she called after them. "I know George will. God be with you, gentlemen."

Weary of fruitless protest, weary of waiting for faint promises of reconciliation, Congress decided that action was necessary. First of all the country needed a commander-in-chief for the army near Boston. It was from New England that the suggestion came that this general should be Washington, a Virginian. Nothing, argued John Adams, would unite the colonies so much as to have a southerner commanding northern soldiers. Unanimously Congress voted for him.

Modestly he accepted the appointment saying, "I beg it may be remembered by every gentleman in this room that I this day declare, with the utmost sincerity, I do not think myself equal to the command I am honored with. As to pay, sir," he turned to Hancock, the president, "I beg leave to assure the Congress that I do not wish to make any profit from it. I will keep an exact account of my expenses. Those I doubt not, they will discharge and that is all I desire."

To his wife he wrote,

"You may believe me, my dear Patsy, when I assure you in the most solemn manner that, so far from seeking this appointment, I have used every endeavor in my power to avoid it. But as it has been a kind of destiny that has thrown me upon this service, I shall hope that my undertaking it is designed to answer some good purpose."

In June he started north to take command of the army. All along the way men and women pressed forward to see him. They held their children up to look upon him. With new strength and courage they turned back to their work, for beneath that stately form and military bearing they saw an honesty and sincerity of purpose that stirred their hearts to patriotism.

The task to which Washington had set his hand was gigantic. Against the thirteen colonies was England, the mightiest empire in the world. She had naval and military powers unequalled. She had a record of centuries of triumph and conquest. Counting eight hundred thousand slaves the colonists were less than four million souls and of these a goodly number were loyal to the king. Congress had no power to prosecute the war vigorously and supply all that was needed. There was no team work. There was no national spirit.

Under the famous elm tree in Cambridge Washington drew his sword and took command of the army. From that moment the Revolution was embodied in him. In spite of defeats and trials, in spite of every obstacle he carried it through to final victory.

First of all he must make an army. The soldiers were brave and enthusiastic, but wholly undisciplined. He taught and trained his men, he fixed the rank of his officers and soothed their jealousies, he hunted the country over for powder, hiding his shortage by a Yankee trick of barrels of sand that were merely topped with powder. More than once before his very eyes the army melted away, for Congress enlisted troops for only three months or six.

The seizing of Dorchester Heights was number one of Washington's great successes. Wagons and timber, tools and bales of hay his men moved at night up to the hills overlooking Boston. Almost by magic their defenses grew. In the morning the British saw ramparts and cannon on Dorchester Heights. Rubbing their eyes they looked again.

"It's like the work of Aladdin's genie," exclaimed one of the redcoats.

Remembering their heavy losses at Bunker Hill they waited instead of attacking. Soon shot and shell sang over Boston. Staying would mean destruction. Quickly they took to their ships and sailed away to Halifax, leaving behind them two hundred cannon and all their military supplies. Without loss of life or property a brilliant victory was won.

An equally brilliant move Washington made in New Jersey the following December. In pitchy darkness, through grinding ice the Americans crossed the Delaware river. In a blinding snow they marched nine miles to Trenton. So badly equipped was the army that many of the men nearly barefoot marked their journey by bloody footprints.

"Our guns are wet," an officer reported to Washington as they neared the town.

"Use the bayonet. Trenton must be taken."

Dawn found the little army stumbling along, marching with heads bent against the driving sleet. The steaming horses strained at the cannon and floundered in the mud at every step. Splashing, trampling the men slipped along in the slush with grim determination. They said not a word, but now and

again looked at their officers marked with bits
of white paper on their hats.

At eight o'clock that Christmas morning the
town was suddenly awakened by the sound of
firing.   The Hessian soldiers were still asleep
after their prolonged festivities on Christmas
Eve.   They had no time to form in line of
battle as their colonel ordered.

The American guns were wheeled into position.   With fatal precision they were fired into
the huddled ranks of the enemy.   The colonel
fell mortally wounded.   His regiment broke
and fled.   Confusion reigned.   All exits from
the town were blocked.   The bewildered Hessians were caught as in a net.   Their officers
raised their hats on their swords in token of
surrender.

In less than an hour the battle of Trenton
was over.   With captured horses and cannon,
with almost a thousand prisoners, Washington recrossed the Delaware.   In twenty-four
hours he was safe again in his own camp.
Success two.

To punish and capture Washington after
this battle came Lord Cornwallis with an army
of eight thousand.   Not far from the American position they camped for the night.

"At last we've run down the old fox," Cornwallis said to his officers, "and we'll bag him in the morning."

But Washington left a few men to keep his camp fires burning brightly and to work noisily with their shovels as if they were throwing up earthworks. By a roundabout road he led his whole force to Princeton. In the morning he attacked the British rear and in a sharp fight crushed it.

Cornwallis could scarcely believe his eyes when he saw that the fox had vanished. He could scarcely believe his ears when he heard, carried far on the cold, still, winter air, the sound of firing at Princeton.

"This three weeks' campaign," said Frederick the Great of Prussia, accounted the greatest soldier of that day, "is the most brilliant of the century. The young American general has opened a fresh chapter in the art of war. England hasn't a man to match him."

The fourth great success of Washington was in Virginia, the last act of the play. He issued false orders for a vigorous movement against New York and let them fall into the hands of the British general. Then cutting loose from the Hudson by forced marches he went to Yorktown. With an army of sixteen thousand, counting the French under Lafayette, he pressed Cornwallis hard.

The French fleet prevented escape by sea. Day by day the lines were drawn tighter about the besieged town. With pickaxes and shovels the Americans threw up entrenchments behind which they crept nearer and nearer the imprisoned garrison. Night and day Washington kept them at this work. Every detail he supervised so that no time, no strength was wasted.

Two of the British redoubts were taken by storm. Cornwallis made heroic attempts to break through the lines. Once his scheme was foiled by a terrific storm, again by the watchfulness of the Americans. His defenses were battered to the ground. Beneath the steady fire of fifty guns the town itself was crumbling to pieces.

One morning a red-coated drummer boy mounted one of the ramparts. Beside him appeared an officer with a white flag. Firing ceased instantly. Blindfolded the flag-bearer brought to Washington a proposal to surrender. On the nineteenth of October. the day that we call Lafayette Day, Cornwallis surrendered to the fox he had expected to bag near the Delaware.

If his successes numbered only four Washington had to his credit defeats as great as victories, with results as important. His retreat across New Jersey, the failures at Brandywine and Germantown which kept the English so occupied that they could send no help to Burgoyne at Saratoga, living through that terrible winter at Valley Forge, meeting with calm dignity the Conway plot against him, achieving a half-success at Monmouth where the traitorous Lee ordered a retreat and upset the well-laid plans for the day—these were disasters which proved his skill in war.

Some writers say indeed that Washington's greatest victory came in the trying months between Yorktown and peace. The unpaid army was discontented and restless. A meeting of officers was called to make a plan to force Congress to help them. A weak man would have kept silent. A rash one would have suppressed the meeting. Neither rash nor weak Washington quietly took control of the movement. Time and place for the gathering he announced.

"Gentlemen," he said opening a paper and

taking out his glasses, "you see I have grown both gray and blind in the service of my country."

Then he read an appeal to their patriotism, begging them to remain loyal and obedient, true to their past. The scheme was abandoned. The officers swore allegiance to the government.

The army loved Washington and believed in him. They wanted him to command in peace as well as war. They proposed that he become dictator or king. He had fought not to win place or glory for himself, but for a great cause. He refused these suggestions. With the treaty of peace he resigned his commission and returned quietly to "Mount Vernon." Glad he was to be a private citizen again.

But during the next four years he did not hold aloof from public affairs. Anxiously he watched the feeble confederation breaking to pieces. Instead of one nation there threatened to be thirteen weak states, each jealous of the other twelve.

What few men of that time dreamed of Washington foresaw—instead of thirteen colonies a great nation enlarging to the westward, crossing the mountains, reaching to the mouth of the Mississippi. He was an empire builder, but this should be an empire of the people enjoying liberty and independence. This national view he put before the leaders of the country by letter over and over again.

A call was sent out for a convention to meet at Philadelphia and form a more perfect union among the states. Washington was one of the Virginia delegates. Unanimously he was chosen president. Four to seven hours a day, from May to September the members worked, considering all the plans brought forward for a government that would give the country order instead of chaos.

The constitution they drafted was forwarded to Congress and then sent to the thirteen states to be ratified. Early in 1789 came the election of the first president. All eyes were turned to George Washington. When the votes were counted every one was for him.

He thought himself a general, not a statesman. "I'd rather be on my farm than emperor of the world," he said. But the nation was calling him and he obeyed though it meant tasks more difficult than he had faced during the long war. As he had borne the burden of the Revolution he now took up the burden of bringing a new government into existence.

Standing on the balcony of Federal Hall in Wall Street, New York City he took the oath of office.

"Long live George Washington, president of the United States!" cried Robert R. Livingston who as chancellor of the state had given him the oath. From the crowd a great shout went up while cannon announced the first inaugural ceremonies.

The new government, said Washington, must win the respect of the people as well as their loyalty. It must be administered with firmness, with prudence, with consideration. It must be dignified, neither haughty nor servile. It must have as its advisers the best brains of the nation. He selected as his cabinet Hamilton and Jefferson, Knox and Randolph—all young and very able men with special knowledge of the work they were to do.

At the cost of his popularity for the time Washington kept peace with England and later with France. Twenty years without war, he argued, were necessary for a nation that was still weak, like a sick man convalescing after a long illness.

How great was the total of his twenty years

of public service! As commander-in-chief he won the liberties of the country. As president he laid deep and strong the foundations on which a mighty nation could be solidly built. He made the new government respected in other lands.

For a century and more Americans have kept his birthday and have called him "father." Nor is his influence bounded by the United States. From him Lafayette learned the principles of liberty and free government that France made use of in forming her republic. San Martin read the story of his life and was inspired to the mighty effort that established three republics in South America. Simon Bolivar impressed with the spirit of Washington won the liberty of five countries.

The nation's capital city, a great state in the west, many counties and cities bear his name. For the beautiful, tall shaft that forms his monument in the District of Columbia a stone was sent by each state in the Union.

"First in war," said Light Horse Harry Lee; then a greater thing, "first in peace;" and greatest of all, "first in the hearts of his countrymen."

THE CHILDREN'S PARADISE

THE THIRD OF MARCH
THE FIFTH OF MAY

"There!" exclaimed Takumi-San as he closed the bronze door of the *godown*, "that's the last of the honorable dolls."

He turned from the black, fireproof building, handed several more packages to the servants and followed them into the largest room of the house. It was really three rooms thrown together, with the paper walls and screens pushed back.

Since the children went off to bed two hours ago father and mother have been busily at work. Around two sides of the room the servants put up shelves like flights of steps, so that every object would show to the best advantage. The mother covered them with scarlet cloth and decorated them with flowers, here a spray of azalea in a porcelain jar and on the other side cherry blossoms in a beautiful bowl.

On the raised platform under a painted

silken scroll, the place of honor, she put the effigies of the Mikado and his wife. Very old these dolls are, for they belonged to her great-great-grandmother. Very precious they are, so precious that they aren't kept in the house, but in the *godown* at the end of the garden, where neither fire nor earthquake can harm them during all the year. Very beautiful they are too, dressed in the antique costume of the court, gorgeous robes stiff with silver and gold embroidery and brilliant in color.

One by one, handling them most carefully, Takumi-San and a trusted servant unwrap the numerous parcels and pass the precious contents up to the mother. On the shelves she arranges the Mikado's possessions—all tiny, all beautiful. There are all the articles used by their imperial majesties—the furniture needed to deck a royal palace; a splendid lacquered table service, complete with trays and bowls, with saké pots, rice buckets and tea cups; bullock carts, the carriages of old Japan; and for the empress all kinds of toilet articles —high combs and gilded flowers for her hair, mirrors, and special utensils for blackening the teeth and shaving the eyebrows, two customs that used to be followed.

In front of the lacquered thrones the father places the five court musicians in their splendid robes of office, each with a miniature instrument.   On the lower shelves are still other dolls—generals and soldiers and porters, nobles and tall princes with impassive faces, dressed in stiff, white clothes, 'riksha men, dancers, all in the costume of a long past day; and a mother doll with her baby on her back, inside the blue kimono, its head sticking out over her shoulder exactly as live babies are carried on the sunny streets of Tokio.

"How delighted Maru will be tomorrow!" the mother says.   "Here are the honorable dolls we bought for her on her first third of March.   Eight years ago that was, and now she's such a big girl and wears a wide, stiff *obi* (sash) of shining brocade, tied with a huge bow.   And there are my first dolls that my father chose for me, and the furniture that belongs with them.   That pair was my grandmother's.   Yes, if Maru cares for them lovingly and reverently and takes them with her to her new home when she's married and hands them on to her little daughter, it won't be long before our children's children have nearly as many dolls as there are in the prince's collection."

"Yes," agrees Takumi-San. "Now look! here's the pair I chose for the new girl-baby." He opens a parcel carefully wrapped in silk paper. "They're not made of wood like common dolls. They're enameled clay. Here's her tea set and furniture, and the dolls' clothes —four kimonos apiece, and these wadded ones embroidered with plum blossoms to match the baby's name.

"For it's little Umé's first feast of dolls. We must celebrate it for her. Of course we want to start her collection with specially nice dolls. Just look at this little jinrikisha!" He sets down the tiny two-wheeled cart with a man in a blue blouse to draw it. "And that bundle is bedding—tiny wooden pillows, green mosquito curtains, and a pair of silk quilts—all the things that little Umé herself has. Last of all, for their meals this table," and he unwraps a piece of inlaid ebony four inches square.

"What did you buy for Maru?" asks the mother after she has examined the baby's presents.

"Here it is—see!"

Package after package the father unrolls. On the lowest shelf he sets out a country house with gardens and farm, with a tiny lake and pine trees, complete to the last details of brass fire-box and charcoal basket, of chrysanthemums and smiling gardeners.

At last after hours of work dolls and furniture, dishes and toys are arranged. Everything is ready for the great feast. Tomorrow the third of March is the greatest day of the year for their two little girls. And for the parents no trouble is too great if it will but add to their happiness.

"Ohayo, ohayo," (Good morning) says Maru early the next morning as she greets her father and mother and kneels before them, bowing till her forehead touches the floor. *"Ohayo,"* she repeats reverently to the effigies of the emperor and empress in their gorgeous clothes.

How many, many dolls there are to be examined and admired! Dolls that had belonged to her mother and grandmother and great-grandmother, dolls that have been in the family over a hundred years! Little dolls only four inches high, big dolls that measure four feet! Dolls that are triumphs of art, whose makers took no account of labor or time! Dolls that walk or dance, baby dolls that creep, dolls, dolls, everywhere! They were not made to be handled carelessly and broken, for the Japanese think that if many generations love a doll it may have a soul loved into it.

For a week or more Maru and her girl friends have seen the gay toy shops filled with dolls and playthings for girls. Not a boyish toy was to be seen. There are complete houses for dolls, with painted screens and scrolls for the wall, dresses of rich material, and every article a Japanese doll could need or desire. Some of these toys are very cheap, for even the poorest coolies celebrate this feast and buy in the toy shops for their daughters. Some are very costly, made by hand, of lacquer or porcelain, of gold or silver, of silk and satin. Many of them are very, very beautiful. In the houses of some of the nobles a doll collection is worth a fortune.

One of the favorite dolls of Maru, because it's her favorite story, is the effigy of Kato Kiyomasa, a celebrated warrior who lived about 1600. He carries a miniature spear to remind the children how single-handed he slew a wild tiger in Korea, while he was leading the Japanese soldiers to victory.

But her brother likes best the four samurai, warriors with two swords apiece. He begs their father to tell them once more the tale of the forty-seven Ronins who avenged their lord at Yedo.

"Oh!" cries Maru walking about the room and gazing from prime minister to a noble with his retainers, from the empress to the mythological Raiko, the giant-killer of Japan, "this is better than history lessons at school! Why, here in our own house we can see just how these great persons looked and how they dressed and what they owned." She bends low before the Mikado and adds, "And it tells us to be loyal to our emperor."

With deep and graceful bows she brings to their majesties tiny lacquered trays with their meal of dried rice and sweets, of cake and saké. A special saké this is, brewed for this feast day, a thick, white wine made out of pounded rice.

All day long the little girl plays with these marvelous dolls and their belongings. In her toy kitchen where she has every utensil needed to cook the finest of Japanese feasts, she prepares and serves them sumptuous meals. She pours out their tea and gives them each five cups—the number that signifies special honor. She dresses and undresses some of them. She rolls up their quilts and puts away the tiny wooden pillows on which they sleep. Every action of her mother she mimics, in the most polite and formal manner. Such a wonderful day it is!

This feast of the third of March dates far, far back to the time when the emperor and empress were never seen by the people, but only by a few favored courtiers. The loyal Japanese made images of them, dressed in robes of state, surrounded by all the luxury and pomp due to their rank. In the spring when the cherry trees blossomed these images were displayed throughout the land. Eagerly the people gave them homage, for they believed the Mikado was descended from the god-kings who once ruled over the country.

Watching his little daughter serve the royal dolls and the old Kioto nobles, Takumi-San says to his wife, "It's a marvelous day, this feast of dolls. It makes every Japanese child loyal to the Mikado."

"Yes," she replies, "but it does something

more. It interests a girl in housekeeping. It's a training in ceremony and etiquette. Only think how much of etiquette and ceremony our little Maru will have to observe when she grows up! She'll learn more quickly, because of this third of March, how to prepare food and drink and serve them to grownup people in the neatest and politest way. Yes, you're right. This is the day of days for Japanese daughters."

For three days the honorable dolls will stay in the house for the family and their friends to enjoy the exhibition. Then they'll be packed away, each in a wrapping of heavy, silken paper, and the parcels put into the *go-down* for safe keeping.

Other dolls Maru has, any number of them, to play with all during the year. Dearly she loves them and great fun she has in taking care of them. But the honorable dolls that are taken out for this festival are her precious and prized possessions.

Father and mother, baby sister and Maru's brother Yoshi all have some share in the feast of dolls and its splendid exhibition. But it is primarily a girls' day. To balance it the boys have a day of their own. It comes some two months later after the March winds and all the fun with kites; where in all the world are there such wonderful kites as in Japan—singing kites and fighting kites, kites like dragons or eagles or butterflies or babies? On the fifth of May comes the boys' festival which they call "the feast of flags."

Does it mean the flag, the sweet iris which grows on the river's edge and along the sides of the swampy rice-fields, which is used in Japan for decorations of many kinds? Or does it mean the white flag with the rising sun, the standard of old Japan?

On the fifth of May, say the old legends, an evil-disposed ogre named Oni comes down from the heavens to bring some great harm to little boys. Only one thing he fears—sharp swords. Japanese lads go down to the river or to a rice-field, and pick the long, sword-shaped leaves of the iris. Everywhere they use it on this feast day. They place it on the table. They festoon it about the house. They hang it along the eaves. They wear it on their heads with the sharp leaves projecting from their foreheads like horns. For all he is an ogre, Oni is a great coward. He's afraid of

horned boys. He's afraid to enter a house
with swords hanging from the eaves. Thus a
handful of green leaves frightens him away
on this Japanese holiday.

Yesterday Takumi-San put up a tall bamboo pole in front of his house. Up and down
the street his neighbors were placing poles.

"For the baby boy who has come to my
house since the last feast of flags," says the
father who lives next door.

"For my only son," says Yoshi's father
proudly.

"For my four boys," adds the father across
the street as he puts up a fourth pole.

This morning as soon as the boys said
"Ohayo," and ate their rice with their ivory
chopsticks they ran outdoors to put up the
flags. Everywhere flags must fly today—
flags of paper, of cotton cloth, of silk; flags
with family crests; flags of Japan; flags with
curious designs.

From the tops of the bamboo poles float
perhaps the queerest flags of all. They are
made of paper or cotton cloth. They are of
every size and color—blue or red or gray, but
all of one shape—the shape of a fish called
carp. The breeze quickly fills out their hol-

low bodies. In the spring wind they flap their tails and wriggle their fins and squirm and dart and flop about in the most natural manner.

For every son, a carp. The younger the boy, the larger the fish. The strange flags swell and rise, shrink and fall as the breeze takes or leaves them. The sheen of their scales glints in the sunlight. The streets are alive with these quaint boys' banners. They make a fluttering, rustling wave of bright color that floats over the city.

What does the carp mean to Japanese boys? It can swim against the current. It can leap over waterfalls. Every time a lad looks at his carp he says to himself, "I must be like that—unconquerable! I must mount over every difficulty. When I see my fish struggling with the breeze, the symbol of perseverance and success in life, I hope I'll struggle with everything that opposes me. Only thus can I win fame and honor."

But on this day of days Yoshi and his friends do more than look at the carp and resolve to swim against the current. For weeks the shops have been gay with toys for boys, just as in March they showed only dolls and girls' playthings. Heroes of old Japan, soldiers and famous warriors and wrestlers—these are the images in the shops now. Many of the models are clad in armor. Their horses are richly caparisoned, pawing the ground as if impatient for the battle. Helmets and swords are for sale too, bows and arrows, horns and drums and trumpets, standards and spears and coats of mail.

In Yoshi's house there's an exhibition of warrior dolls with flags and banners. Beside each hero is his crest. In front of them are all kinds of weapons. The food offered them is rice dumplings wrapped in oak leaves, because the oak like the carp is the emblem of strength and endurance.

Each gay toy warrior, each bright standard has its tale of glory. Stories of these noble ancestors the fathers tell their sons to sow the seeds of self-reliance, of belief in the invincible power of their country. For courage and loyalty are the inheritance of every Japanese boy. Hearing these stories Yoshi and his friends resolve to grow up to be worthy of the brave men who lived before them.

This feast of the fifth of May, Takumi-San says, goes all the way back to the thirteenth century. For seven years Japan had been greatly troubled by expeditions sent against her by Kublai Khan—yes, the same Kublai Khan who was Marco Polo's friend. In 1281 another great army invaded the Mikado's empire. Several battles were fought, but the Japanese could not win a decisive victory. Then as if in answer to their prayers a mighty storm arose. The fleet of the enemy was scattered. A last desperate attack the soldiers of the Mikado made. Their foe was completely annihilated. Of a hundred thousand invaders only three escaped to tell their story.

"The storm was a miracle!" cried the Japanese. "The gods intervened to save our country. Let us have a lasting memorial of this wonderful victory. The fifth of May shall be a holiday." For more than six hundred years it has been kept by the boys of Japan.

Among all the soldier dolls Yoshi likes particularly the figures of Shoki-Sama, the strong man who could conquer Oni; of Yoshitsune, the marvelous fencer and general, and his giant retainer; of Jingu Kogo, the brave warrior empress who, lest the troops should be discouraged, concealed from the army the death of her husband, put on armor and led a great campaign against Korea; and Iyeyasu, the maker of Yedo, whom the Japanese consider the greatest ruler the country has ever obeyed, and beside him his famous charger whose tomb is near his master's in the solemn pines of Nikko; and Toyotomi Hedeyoshi, the greatest adventurer and perhaps the greatest general in the history of Japan, with his unique standard of a bright yellow gourd.

Yoshi listens breathlessly as he hears once more the story of this man, born in the lowest rank of the people, who became regent of the land, who brought about peace after two hundred years of strife, a peace that lasted for two centuries; who when challenged to single combat had no standard to carry on to the field and tore up by the roots a gourd growing by the roadside and used it as a banner.

Eagerly the lad answers the questions his father puts to test his knowledge of Japanese history. The example of these heroes he too must follow. He must be brave in battle. He must be persevering in difficulties. Thus only can a Japanese boy repay all that he owes to his father, to the emperor and to Japan.

Takumi-San gives his son presents on this feast day, just as he did to Maru and the baby.

But now the gifts are a sword and a set of toys—an arsenal with generals, soldiers on foot and on horse, flags and banners, tents and racks for arms.

For this festival Yoshi and his friends have several favorite games. In one they form themselves into a *daimiyo's* procession (a *daimiyo* was a native prince, in the olden days, his followers were the samurai). They choose officers and runners to clear the highroad. They imitate to the last detail the pomp of the *daimiyo's* train. In the shops the boys can buy all the equipment for such a procession.

There used to be a very popular game which represented a war between two noble families, rivals in feudal times. All the lads of a town or district were divided into two parties. Sometimes there were several hundred of them, marshalled in squadrons as in an army. The Heiki had white flags, the Genji red. Each boy carried a bamboo sword. On his head he fastened a flat, round piece of earthenware.

The signal was given. The battle commenced. Slash, slash! went the toy swords. The object was to break the earthen disks on the heads of the enemy. Any soldier whose helmet was demolished had to retire from the field defeated, for the broken disk represented a broken skull.   The noble whose men had the greater number of disks unbroken won the day.

Always the contest was exciting.   Often boys were seriously hurt in this mimic warfare. Now this game that belongs to the fifth of May is forbidden by the government.

Instead the Heiki and Genji have a different kind of contest.   Each boy has a flag, white or red.   In the battle the object is to seize flags from the foe.   A boy who loses his must leave the field.   The side with the most flags at the end of the struggle is the victor.

When all the fun is over Yoshi and his friends are tired out.   For absolute enjoyment do the boys of any other country get so much out of their holidays as Japanese boys from this feast of flags?   It's worth being tired for!

Japan is called the land of the rising sun, the land of cherry blossoms, of the chrysanthemum.   But its best name is the children's paradise.   In no other country are there so many fine toys and games for boys and girls. In no other land do the parents give so much time and thought to their children's holidays, or share so fully in their pleasures. Where else do they celebrate with a special day for the girls and a special day for the boys?

"*O-Sayonara!*" (Goodbye) call Yoshi and Maru, "*O-Sayonara!*"

THE TORCH BEARER

MARCH THE SEVENTEENTH

Green! Green!

Green in the shops, you say. Green candies and green clothes and green carnations and little green flags. And men selling something they call shamrock on the street corner. And you young folks want to know the meaning of it all. So you've come to me because you saw me marching in the parade this morning, wearing a sash of green?

Well, I'll tell you the best I can. But a poor best I fear me it will be. For while it's easy enough to tell the story of this holiday, how can an old man put into words all it means, all it stands for to Ireland and to her children all over the world?

But to begin now, and it's an Irish bull I begin with, St. Patrick isn't Irish at all. He's British, born on the west coast of Scotland, toward the end of the third century. His father was a magistrate in the Roman colony near the mouth of the river Clyde, not so far from Glasgow. His mother was a niece of St. Martin of Tours.

The father taught the boy   that a Roman citizen should know. The mother taught him to be courteous and knightly, for she brought from sunny France many a memory of courtly manners. So Patrick grew up learning various things not known in that wild, savage, northern land. But the chief of them was a knowledge of the Christian faith. Psalms he had to learn and many prayers. Sometimes these lessons seemed dull and uninteresting.

"I wonder now," he would think, "if it isn't pleasanter to be a heathen than a Christian? For they have no psalms to learn, no prayers to recite."

"Some day you'll think differently," answered his gentle mother. "What you call dull tasks will be like apples of gold in pictures of silver."

One stormy night when the lad Patrick was sixteen years old pirates from Ireland burst into the farmhouse where the Romans sat before the glowing peat fire. Without warning they were attacked. Bravely they fought and with no thought of fear. Outnumbered, overpowered they were killed, or captured and bound hand and foot.

"To the boats!" cried the pirate captain. "Handle the lad carefully, my men," he added pointing to Patrick at the end of the row of prisoners. "He's strong and will bring a good price on the other side. No, no, leave the women here."

Through the long dark night the boat tossed on the stormy sea. When morning came Patrick found himself in Ireland. The pirates sold him to a man who lived in county Antrim. And he was sent to feed his master's swine.

On the mountains, in the forest, in snow and rain the young slave lived for six long years. Often he was hungry. Often he was bitterly cold. It was a life to test his endurance, strong and hardy as he was. Rest and leisure? None for him. A slave's tasks are never finished. Snow on the ground? He must drive out his pigs and find acorns for them. Frequently he spent the night on the hillside though a biting wind swept over the mountains.

One thing he had in plenty—time to think. He thought of his home, of his parents, and of

the dull lessons his mother had made him learn.
Little by little they came back to him. In
the psalms, in the prayers that he now recited
over and over he found many a word of comfort. They were indeed like apples of gold in
pictures of silver.

Patrick made good use of these long months
of slavery. He learned the manners and customs and language of the people of Ireland.
He learned to see beauty in the common things
around him. You know the story of how he
was asked, years afterward, to explain the
Trinity—three persons in one—and how he
stooped down and from the grass at his feet
plucked a leaf of the delicate, little, green
shamrock and used its three leaves growing
from one stem to illustrate the mystery?

One night when he was resting in the shelter
of a rock he fell asleep. In his dream he heard
a voice say, "You shall soon return to your
home. Behold, a ship is ready."

It was the voice of an angel, Patrick thought.
He set out for the seashore at once. After
many a weary mile he found a ship with sails
already set to begin its voyage to Britain.

"No," cried the captain angrily, "begone!
I'll take no runaway slave!"

Sorrowfully Patrick turned away and trudged up the road. But the captain changed his mind and sent a sailor after him.

"Come, we'll take you on trus. You can work out your passage."

Fainter and fainter grew the Irish coast. Three days later the ship reached land, but not near the river Clyde. Across a strange, desolate country they had to travel. Day by day their supply of food grew less. Must they starve to death?

"Christian," said the captain, "I've often watched you at your prayers. Pray for us now, for we are starving."

"I will," answered Patrick, "but you too must have faith."

He knelt down and prayed. Suddenly in the woods there was a rushing, tearing sound. A herd of wild boars swept by. The sailors gave chase and soon killed enough to give them food for weeks.

After twenty-seven days of wild adventure Patrick reached home again. Picture the joy and happiness of his arrival! All his hardships, all his troubles were forgotten. But he could not be again the careless lad of sixteen. He was a man and must do a man's work in the world.

"Yes," agreed his mother. "But I beg of you, do it here. Never leave us, now that we have found you so wonderfully."

For a while that was Patrick's sole desire, to stay in his dear home. Then one night as he slept an angel came to him carrying a bun-- dle of letters. On the first was written, "The voice of the Irish." As he read the words he heard a call, the voices of many people who dwelt by the western ocean, "Come and dwell with us! We pray thee, holy youth, walk among us as before!"

His eyes were dimmed with tears. He could no longer see the letter held out to him and he awoke.

Those people near the western ocean were poor and untaught. They were heathen and had never heard of God. Patrick made up his mind to spend his life preaching to them. With the torch of God's love in his hand he would spread abroad the glorious light of Christianity in every corner of dark Ireland.

His friends and relatives opposed this plan. They made Patrick great offers to detain him.

They tried to frighten him with talk of the dangers of that savage land. But for riches and honors he cared nothing. His one desire was to carry his message to the Irish people. By day he thought of Ireland. By night he dreamed of her green and fertile shores.

But he was too wise to go unprepared. For such a mission years of study were needed. Into France and Italy Patrick journeyed. At Tours he stayed with his mother's uncle. From the good St. Martin's hands he received the habit of a monk. It was the pope Celestine, say the old books, who consecrated him bishop and charged him to convert the people of Ireland.

In the year 432 the lad who had been a slave and swineherd returned. Not alone he went, but with a train of clergy and helpers. Books and priestly vestments he had and his pastoral staff; and learning and a loving heart, and that was best of all.

At Wicklow they landed. The first person they met was a lad tending swine. Terrified he fled away through the woods to his master.

"Pirates!" he cried. "Pirates are landing at the bay!"

But when the man summoned his followers

and marched down to the beach he saw only
a group of unarmed folk.

"Friends and not enemies they are," he
called back to his soldiers after he had talked
earnestly with Patrick. "Put up your weapons!"

Now it was in the spring that this torch-
bearer returned to Ireland. But the glad season of Easter had no meaning for the people.
They worshiped the sun which was putting
winter to flight and changing buds to blossoms.
In its honor every year their priests, the
Druids, held a great festival at Tara where
lived the fierce King Laoghaire. On the day
before all fires were put out. On pain of
death no man could kindle one until the king's
great festal beacon should be lighted on the
hill of Tara.

When Patrick heard of this gathering of
the people and their priests, and that the king
himself would be there, it seemed a splendid
opportunity. Swiftly he traveled across hill
and dale. On Easter Eve he reached the hill
of Slane, a dozen miles from the mouth of the
river Boyne.

The whole land was wrapped in darkness.
Not a fire, not a light was to be seen. Over

Tara was a solemn blackness. The night was cold. Patrick started a fire and sat watching the little tongues of flame as they shot up higher and higher.

The white-robed Druids and the king saw the glowing light. Astonished and angry Laoghaire asked, "Who has dared do this thing?"

"None of thy subjects surely, my lord king," said the priests. "The commands are most strict. Gold and silver could not save the life of a man who disobeyed. It is an enemy."

"What does it mean then?"

"The old prophecies say, if this fire be not extinguished tonight it will never be extinguished, but will overtop all our fires. And he that kindled it will overturn thy kingdom."

"He shall not challenge us thus," cried the king. "We will go forth and punish this bold stranger."

There was heard the shouting of men and the stamping of horses while the royal chariots were made ready. Over the dark, silent hillside went king and priests, till they came nearer and nearer to the fire burning on the hill of Slane.

"Go not within the line of that magic light," urged the Druids. "Let a messenger fetch him forth."

"You say well. We will wait here. Rise not when he comes, lest he should think we seek to honor him."

They sat down to wait the return of the messenger. Soon Patrick came toward them, outlined against the flickering fire. As he approached the group sat silent, the warriors resting their chins on the rims of their great shields, looking grim and terrible in the flaring light.

Forgetting the king's order one of the pages rose to his feet in reverent greeting. Raising his hand Patrick blessed the lad. And years later he became bishop of Slane.

"Who are you?" questioned Laoghaire. "What is your errand here?"

"I am a torch bearer. I bring light to this dark land. I bring peace and good will. Hear my message, I pray."

"Slay him!" commanded the king.

Before his followers could obey a violent tempest arose. In fright the horses ran over the plain. The chariots were swept away and destroyed. Confused and terrified, the people turned upon each other fiercely. After struggle and bloodshed they fled. Only the king and one other remained. Alone, unarmed Patrick stood before them.

"Come to Tara tomorrow," said Laoghaire, "and speak before the court."

This was what Patrick most desired. Robed in white, wearing his mitre and carrying his staff the priest appeared at Tara. Unafraid in the presence of king and court he explained the leading points in the teachings of Christianity. A new and wonderful message it was, of love and mercy and forgiveness. Such words the Irish had never heard before. Laoghaire gave permission for the newcomers to go safely through his dominions to teach and to preach.

What a glad Easter for the new bishop, for the slave who had tended swine in that land!

Up and down through the country ruled by Laoghaire Patrick went with his Christian teachings. Into Connaught he journeyed and won over the seven sons of the king and twelve thousand of his subjects. To the far west he went and north to the most distant point on the rocky coast of Antrim, then south to the very end of Munster. Thus his travels formed a cross over Ireland.

Now a wild and rude country it was. The poor people used to worship snakes. No one dared to kill them and the Irish were greatly troubled, the land was so full of the reptiles. Patrick traveled over the land, says the old story, with a drummer marching before him beating the big drum with all his might. The power of the good saint, added to the noise of the drum frightened the snakes. Fast as they could they ran and jumped into the sea. And in the whole of Ireland today you can't find a single living snake!

But once Patrick met up with a monstrous serpent that feared him not a whit. Instead of running away it lay right across his path. What should he do? He hunted around till he found a big box with a strong cover. With many a soft word—for though he wasn't Irish he'd learned the Irish way of speaking—he coaxed the snake to get into the box.

"It's too small to hold me," said the wily creature.

" 'Tis quite large enough," declared Patrick.

At great length they argued the matter.

"I'll show you!   I'll prove the truth of what
I say," cried the serpent angrily.

Slowly, carefully it crawled in and coiled
down.   In a flash the cover was clapped on
tight.   The box was cast into the Irish Sea.

The rest of his life Patrick spent among
these people.   He labored to win over the
chiefs of the land.   Their followers would then
be the more ready to hearken to his message.
He labored to teach the lads.   He could not
forget his own years as a tender of swine.
From him the people learned to believe in God.
Gladly they turned from darkness to the light.

When a chief became a Christian it was the
custom for him to give Patrick a piece of land
on which to build a church.   Near each of the
three   hundred   and   sixty-five   churches   he
founded a school.   In the monasteries he left
disciples to carry on his work.

All who loved learning flocked to these Irish
schools so that they became famous through
western   Europe.   Thither   came   also   the
Druids, the poets and musicians of that age.
But now they tuned their harps in the service of
God.   Beautiful was their music, so beautiful
that it's said the angels of heaven stooped down

to listen. That's why the harp became the badge of Ireland.

And at last after he'd givēn many a year of faithful work and had made the Irish people Christians, in the spring when the shamrocks decked the land with their dainty green Patrick died. Everywhere there was mourning. From the most remote villages priests and people came to pay a last tribute to their master. For twelve days and nights the ceremonies lasted, each group joining as it arrived. The blaze of hundreds of torches made the whole time seem like one continuous day.

Now whether he died on the eighth of March or on the ninth I can not tell. Among the Irish there was great debate. Some insisted on the one day and some held out for the other. At last they decided to add the two together and to have the seventeenth for St. Patrick's day.

For all that he did for her Ireland can never be grateful enough. She chose him for her patron saint. She worships his memory and keeps it green forever. In every Irish family there's sure to be a Patrick or a Patricia.

The world over Irishmen celebrate this day. We parade with music and banners. We wear the green and make speeches in praise of the emerald isle, in honor of our saint. Do you see why?

"TO ARMS! THE REDCOATS ARE COMING!"

THE NINETEENTH OF APRIL

A few years ago about ten o'clock one April night a fourteen-year-old girl crept up the steps of the belfry of Christ Church in Boston. Without pausing to look down on the narrow, crooked streets of the North End, or on the river near by she went about her task. She lighted the two lanterns hanging from her arm. High in the belfry she placed them.

Americans and Italians, Poles and Russians of that crowded tenement neighborhood saw the two gleaming lights and said, "Ah, look! There's the signal!"

Across the river Charles waited a man in colonial dress. The moment the lights flashed out he swung himself on to his good gray horse and rode off into the darkness. From Charlestown to Medford he rode and on to Arlington. Through stretches of green fields and patches of woodland, past trim market gardens and suburban villages, on through the night he went to Lexington and thence to Concord.

To every group he chanced to meet on the highway, to the sleeping people in houses near the road the horseman shouted out his message: "Up and to arms! The regulars are coming!"

In old colonial farmhouses, in modern suburban residences, in beautiful country homes men and women and children sat at the windows watching for that swift rider. They heard the hard galloping of his horse. They heard the exciting words, "To arms! The redcoats are coming!"

And when scarcely drawing rein he had dashed on toward the next village, fathers and mothers turned to their children and told them the story of the ride taken on the eighteenth of April in 1775 by the ancestor of the girl who lighted the lanterns in the old North Church.

The winter of 1774–5 was an exciting time in old Boston town. The colony's quarrel with Parliament and George III grew hotter. Step by step matters were coming to a crisis. The people were determined to have their rights as Englishmen. They would not be taxed unless they had representation in the body that voted their taxes.

Boston had resisted the stamp act. She had thrown the tea into the harbor. Then by the king's orders her port was closed, the assembly dissolved.

Delegates from the various colonies had met at Philadelphia in a Continental Congress and had petitioned the king and Parliament to restore their rights. The answer was the sending of General Gage with four regiments of soldiers to Boston.

Meanwhile the people of Massachusetts organized an assembly of their own. They chose John Hancock, the rich Boston merchant, as president. They made plans for summoning minute-men, as they called those citizens who pledged themselves to be ready to fight at a minute's notice. They began collecting military stores. If the need came they'd be all prepared for war in defense of their liberties.

All that exciting winter the Sons of Liberty in Boston held secret meetings. So many members there were that they were organized in three sections. The one in the North End was led by Dr. Joseph Warren and his right-

hand man was Paul Revere, goldsmith and en-
graver.

It was Revere who formed among the workingmen a patrol that for weeks watched the
movements of British soldiers in the streets of
Boston. Two by two his thirty mechanics
walked up and down every thoroughfare listening, listening. Any news of importance
they brought to the Green Dragon Tavern in
Union Street, "the headquarters of the Revolution," as it came to be called.

In April the air in the North End of Boston was charged with excitement. It was all
the more intense because it was smothered.

The British, the Sons of Liberty knew, had
received orders from London to seize all arms
and ammunition, and to arrest the two arch-
traitors, Samuel Adams and Hancock, and
send them to England. Too well they knew
what that meant—a trial for treason, the
Tower of London and the block. In addition
a price was set upon their heads.

More closely the patrol watched and listened. What were the redcoats planning?
Something out of the ordinary was going on
in their camp.

On Saturday, the fifteenth of the month,

one of Revere's men discovered that the grenadiers and the light infantry had been taken off duty. A second item was reported—all the small boats from the transports had been hauled up for repairs and anchored under the sterns of the men-of-war.

"Plainly," said Paul Revere as he talked over these reports with Dr. Warren, "their troops are making ready to cross over to Charlestown. Are they after the stores at Concord? or after Mr. Hancock and Mr. Adams at Lexington?"

"Perhaps both. At any rate our leaders are in danger. Do you, Revere, go out to Lexington and tell them what you've learned. They're lodging at the parsonage, you know— the Reverend Jonas Clarke's."

So on Sunday Paul Revere mounted his big gray horse and rode out to Lexington. It was only thirteen miles. The big gray steed was strong and fleet. And his rider was a fine horseman, tireless and enduring. By night he was back again.

Now that very Saturday the assembly which had been meeting in Concord adjourned for some weeks. Its committee of safety met on Monday, heard from Adams and Hancock the message brought by Revere, and voted to send away the supplies that had been collected. The musket balls and powder they would not try to hide all in one place. To nine different towns they were sent for the safer keeping. Tents, medicine chests and linen were divided among six villages. Spades and shovels, salt fish and rice were shared with other towns.

Meanwhile back in Boston the Sons of Liberty were certain something was afoot. The *Somerset,* one of the men-of-war, had moved up the bay. Her guns covered the ferry and could cut the patriots off from the other side of the Charles. Getting across might be difficult.

So Paul Revere arranged with a friend that if any large body of soldiers left the city, lanterns should be hung in the brick steeple of Christ Church—the Old North Church they called it even then; for wasn't it the oldest church in Boston, dating back to 1723? One light if the British were to march overland; two if they started by water. From that high steeple the lights would flash the message far away.

Tuesday night the vigilant patrol reported,

"A number of soldiers are moving toward the bottom of the Common."

"Ah!" said Paul Revere to himself, "now we know their plans. Instead of marching round by Boston Neck they'll cross to Charlestown and then go west to Lexington and Concord."

Just at that moment a boy came with a message. Dr. Warren wanted him for an important errand. Paul Revere was not surprised. How many times already he had been the trusted messenger of the committee of safety —in December year before last to New York over frozen roads, with news of the Boston tea party; in June to Philadelphia to ask help from the other colonies when the port of Boston was closed; and again in September he brought from the first Continental Congress a message of approval and advice for the patriots of Massachusetts: Avoid collision with the king's troops, act only on the defensive. All this was running through Revere's mind as he walked to Dr. Warren's. Well, he was ready —as ready as a minute-man.

The doctor too was ready with his instructions.

"William Dawes has already started to Lexington to give warning that the British are coming. He's to go all the way by horseback over Boston Neck. Do you, Revere, cross over to Charlestown and then ride west on this hurry call. One of you may not get through. And if you both succeed, riding by different roads you'll warn that many more of our men. Dawes has the start of you. Best set off at once. You've twenty miles before you."

It was after ten o'clock.

Revere went to his house in North Square, took up his overcoat and boots and walked down to the river. Two good friends rowed him across the Charles. Their oars were muffled so that they did not attract the attention of the watch on the *Somerset,* lying a bit to the west of where they passed. Once ashore Paul Revere got a horse from Deacon Larkin and set out.

Twenty miles it was to Concord and the night was dark. Before he had gone far the keen eyes of this patriot rider saw two British officers on horseback, waiting under a tree. One headed him off, the other rode directly toward him. The deacon's horse was turned short about.

Revere retraced his way for a bit. Then at

a dark spot in the road he struck off at right angles for the Medford highway—not easy going, but he knew the lay of the land. His pursuer got into a clay pond. Soon he had outwitted this enemy patrol.

At Medford the captain of the minute-men was wakened. He rubbed his eyes. Sleepily he heard the message: "The redcoats are coming! To arms!" Then wide awake he stared after the sturdy horseman already galloping up the road, reached for his old musket in the chimney corner and called out his men.

From Medford on Paul Revere stopped at almost every house, shouted out his warning sentence and galloped westward. It was after midnight when he reached the green at Lexington. A little way off, on the North Road, stood the parsonage. The household had just retired, for the three men, Adams and Hancock and the preacher, had talked late—about king and Parliament, about unjust laws and the rights of British subjects.

The hard galloping of the deacon's horse broke the stillness of the night.

"Halt! Who goes there?"

"A friend," answered **Revere**, **"and in a** precious hurry!"

"No noise," cautioned the sentry, one of eight men guarding the house.

"Noise! You'll have noise enough before long. The regulars are coming. They're on the march and will soon be among you."

"Come in, Revere," John Hancock called out recognizing his voice.

Into the parsonage went the goldsmith and told his errand. Hancock reached for his gun and fell to cleaning it.

"I'll join the minute-men," he declared, "and face the enemy. It shall never be said of me that I turned my back upon the British."

"No, no!" argued Adams. "We have other work to do."

"If you stay here," urged Paul Revere, "you're liable to be captured. Lives will be lost. Time will be wasted. Get away from Boston and this neighborhood. Go down to Philadelphia. You'll be needed there."

A half hour's rest the deacon's horse had. Then William Dawes rode up and Revere joined him.

"Suppose I go on to Concord with you," said young Dr. Prescott who had been in Lexington that evening to call on his sweetheart.

"I know the road, every inch of it, and all the houses where you should stop."

Off rode the three to carry their warning. Half way to Concord they ran into a group of ten British officers. They were surrounded and forced into a pasture where the bars were down at one side of the road.

Their only chance of escape lay in separating. Prescott struck spurs to his horse, jumped a stone wall and rode on all the way to Concord, calling out his message as he galloped along.

With two of the British pursuing him Dawes dashed up to an empty farmhouse, slapped his leather breeches loudly and shouted, "Halloo, boys! I've got two of 'em!" Frightened by this Yankee trick the redcoats turned and fled. Dawes too went on to Concord. Both he and Prescott were at the bridge that day.

Revere meanwhile turned to the right across the pasture and made for a little wood. His plan was to jump from his horse and run. From the shadow of the trees came half a dozen British officers on horseback.

"Dismount."

There was nothing for it but to obey.

"What is your name?"

"Revere."

"Paul Revere?"

"Yes."

"Are you an express?"   For so swift messengers were called in colonial times.

"Yes."

"When did you leave Boston?"

He told them, adding, "Your troops ran aground in crossing the river.   Five hundred Americans will be here in a short time, for I alarmed the country all the way up."

With a redcoat leading his horse Paul Revere went back toward Lexington in the midst of the group of British officers.   So many dangerous rides he had taken for the Sons of Liberty, and never before had he been captured.   Would Dawes or Prescott get safely to Concord in time for the minute-men to conceal their supplies and be ready to face the enemy?

Half a mile from the Lexington green they heard a signal gun fired.   The bell was ringing.

"What does that mean?" asked the British in alarm.

They took the deacon's horse and rode hastily away. Their prisoner was free!

Across the fields Revere went and back to the Clarke house. Adams and Hancock were just starting. He went with them for a couple of miles and then returned to Lexington to get a trunk filled with Hancock's papers. As he carried it from the tavern to a place of safety he saw a group of minute-men lining up on the green. But he did not join them. Having carried out his orders he must go back to Boston and report to Dr. Warren.

The alarm bell had rung in Lexington. The minute-men had assembled. The watch on the Boston road reported no British in sight. The night was chilly. Captain Parker dismissed his men with orders to stay within drum call. Those living near by went to their homes. The others gathered in the tavern on the north side of the green.

Suddenly they heard the sound of a galloping horse coming down the Boston road.

"The army of redcoats is half a mile away!" reported the sentinel.

"Beat the drum. To arms! To arms!" cried Parker.

William Diamond, the drummer, wakened the green and hills near by with his warlike sounds. From the tavern, from the houses around, the minute-men came running. Ten rods from the meeting-house Captain Parker drew them up in two long lines—seventy-seven of them counting the three who went into the church for powder.

The east windows of the meeting-house brightened with the rays of the coming sunrise. At the edge of the green appeared the first of the British soldiers. In front of his men rode Major Pitcairn.

"Halt!" he called as he heard Diamond's drum call. "Load! Forward march!"

Almost on the run the redcoats came up. There was a rattle of muskets. There was the tramping of heavy feet. The minute-men saw a dim mass of moving figures coming nearer and nearer. They saw the gleam of musket barrels, the scarlet of uniforms.

"There are so few of us. It's folly to stand here," said one of the patriots to his neighbor.

Captain Parker heard the words and exclaimed, loud enough for his seventy-seven men to hear, "Don't fire unless fired upon.

But if they mean to have a war, let it begin here."

"I will never run," said Jonas Parker to himself.

A hundred feet from the two lines Pitcairn stopped.

"Disperse, you rebels!" he shouted. "Lay down your arms and disperse."

Grim silence greeted him. Not a minuteman moved. Not one laid down his musket.

"Fire!" called the British officer.

Over the heads of the patriots his men fired wildly. Pitcairn was angry.

"Fire at them! at them!"

A second volley. Seven Americans fell. Nine others were wounded. The patriots fired back. Two or more of the British were hit.

Other redcoats came into view. Captain Parker saw that they would surround and capture his little band. They were ten to one. He ordered his men to withdraw.

"I will never run," Jonas Parker had said. He did not retire with the others. Once more he fired, his ammunition in his hat on the ground at his feet. Wounded he fell forward. He struggled to rise, tried to reload and said again, "I will never run." Just where he had stood in the first line of the minute-men, he died on the green at Lexington.

Jonathan Harrington too was wounded by that British volley. Across the green was his home. He staggered toward it, fell, rose and stumbled on. At the door his wife met him. He died in her arms.

The British made a dash for the Clarke house. They failed to find Hancock and Adams. Making a show of victory they gave three cheers, fired a volley, and wheeling about started down the road.

But if Paul Revere had been captured Dawes and Prescott had carried the warning to Concord. Trained through years of warfare with Indians and the French, the minutemen were ready. Messengers were sent toward Lexington and soon after sunrise galloped back with news of the skirmish on the green and of the eight hundred redcoats marching westward. There was hurried consultation.

"Let us stand our ground," advised the minister, Mr. Emerson. "If we die let us die here."

"It will not do for us to begin the war," said

others hesitating. "It would be treason to the king if we resist."

At seven o'clock there was a gleam of red on the Lexington road. Into the village came the British. Colonel Barrett saw that he was outnumbered. He marched his men down to the river and took possession of the bridge and of the slope beyond.

In the center of the town Major Pitcairn sent his men to search for arms and powder. They broke open a few barrels of flour. They spiked three cannon and dumped five hundred pounds of bullets into the millpond. Angry at finding so little they chopped down a liberty pole and set fire to the court-house.

"Shall we let them burn the whole village?" the minute-men began asking each other when they saw the smoke.

"There's a considerable store of ammunition at the Barrett house across the river, sir," reported a British scout.

Two hundred soldiers were sent in search of it.

"Shall we let them burn the town?" the minute-men asked again.

"March!" called out their captain.

In double file they started down the slope. The redcoats were coming toward the bridge. Where now the old gray monument stands they formed in line of battle. The Americans halted at the other end of the bridge, where now you see the statue of the Minute-man with his ready flintlock and powder horn.

For an instant British and patriot farmers faced each other in silence.

Bang! Bang! went two muskets of the enemy.

Then others—bang! bang! bang!

The patriot captain fell. Another minute-man went down, another. The war had begun.

"Fire! For God's sake, fire!" called an American officer.

The first battle of the Revolution spoke its defiance to the king of England. Across the bridge shots flew. Two British soldiers fell. Seven were wounded. Then the firing ceased. Toward the town the redcoats ran. The min-ute-men held the bridge they had defended so valiantly.

For an hour and more the British marched and countermarched in Concord. Their col-onel was uncertain what to do. He had been sent to arrest Adams and Hancock and to destroy the stores. In both tasks he had failed. His troops were hungry and weary, for they'd been on the march since midnight. They were thoroughly alarmed. At last the order was given: "Right about face! To Boston!"

But by this time more and more minute-men had assembled. From Lincoln and Acton, Concord's nearest neighbors, they had come. From all the country round farmers hurried up to help. From both sides, from front and rear they attacked the British. The return changed to a retreat.

Not in a long line as on the Lexington green, but in Indian fashion from behind clumps of trees and stone walls they fired at the redcoats. All the way from Concord the helpless British had to run the gauntlet. By the time they reached Lexington their ammunition began to fail.

There at two o'clock Lord Percy met them with two field pieces and twelve hundred fresh men from Boston, formed in a hollow square. Into this shelter the exhausted troops flung themselves, lying down on the ground with their tongues hanging out of their mouths like those of dogs after a chase. With only a brief rest the homeward march began again.

But even this reinforcement could not save the day. The patriot forces grew so rapidly, as minute-men from thirty of the surrounding towns came up, that the British barely escaped capture. The attacks grew hotter and more frequent. Now and then the redcoats would form, turn their cannon upon the unseen enemy and silence them for the moment. But from the stone walls that were like ready-made breastworks the firing began again as soon as the line of march was resumed.

Panic-stricken the British changed from double-quick to a run. Pell-mell, helter-skelter they stumbled along, all order lost. Like hounds worrying game the patriot farmers hung on the skirts of this twenty-mile retreat, firing at every opportunity for a good shot. Like maddened bees, or like a cloud of hornets they swarmed about the enemy.

"It rained rebels!" one British soldier described the scene.

Exhausted, covered with dust, at sunset the redcoats reached Charlestown. There they were safe under the guns of their men-of-war. They had lost two hundred and seventy-three in killed and wounded.

"They have begun it," Dr. Warren commented to a friend. "That either party can do. And we will end it. That only we can do."

The news of the nineteenth of April was carried by expresses to towns all over New England and southward. From Georgia up to Maine the thirteen colonies were roused to action. The skirmish on the green at Lexington, the fight at the Concord bridge, the twenty-mile battle-front stretching all the way to Charlestown began a contest that lasted for seven years and ended only at Yorktown.

At Lexington and Concord and all along the road to Boston the descendants of the minute-men of 1775 have placed tablets to mark the sites of the eventful happenings of that April night and day. On tavern and house-front, on parsonage and stone walls, on the green, near the bridge you can see them to the number of sixty and more. More than once they have acted out on this New England holiday the placing of the lanterns in Christ Church and the midnight ride of Dawes and Paul Revere. They honor both the horsemen who carried the warning, "The redcoats are coming—to arms!" and the minute-men who heard the message and stood ready with their muskets to fight for liberty.

THE NATION THAT WOULD
NOT DIE

THE THIRD OF MAY

In the king's room in the palace at Warsaw
a little group of patriots met. Quietly the discussion went on. Plainly it was a matter of
great moment, to judge from their earnest, serious faces.

"Do you all then," asked one of the leaders,
"solemnly pledge yourselves not to separate
till our end is accomplished?"

"We do," came the answer. "It is for
Poland."

They left the king's room and went into the
great hall where the meetings of the Diet were
held. The galleries were crowded with spectators. Outside the palace waited thousands
of people who could not gain admission.

The members of the Diet took their places.
Three hundred and fifty-four there were when
all were present; a double number in that
spring of 1791 because when the two years of
the Diet of 1788 were nearly over and their

special business was not completed, it was voted that new deputies should be chosen and added to those already sitting. How absurd it would have been to leave an unfinished task to wholly new hands!

Ordinarily one of the marshals opened a session of the Diet. Today King Stanislas himself performed this office. The spectators leaned over from the galleries to see the better. What a fine-looking, handsome man their king was!

The first business of the day was a report from the committee of foreign affairs. Close attention the members paid as it was read by the marshal. Danger threatened the republic of Poland! Without a dissenting vote the committee prophesied a second partition of the country.

Instantly there was the greatest excitement in the Diet. Another partition of Poland? Would nothing satisfy their powerful and ambitious neighbors, Russia and Prussia and Austria?

Only a few years ago, in 1772, Poland had been forced to agree to a treaty which robbed her of a third of her territory and four millions of her people. Immediately Russian troops

had been stationed in the land. Indignantly
the proud Poles chafed under this foreign dic-
tation. But it had one good result. It con-
vinced the nobles that reform was needed if
their country was ever to be really free. From
this time the anti-Russian feeling grew and
grew.

A majority in the Diet wanted reform. But
they found it by no means easy to agree as to
the details. Jealously some of the members
clung to their old privileges. The debates
were endless. A doubled Diet did not shorten
the discussions. Indeed it meant doubled eloquence and increased disputes. After three
years the business was not finished.

So the little group of patriots had met in the
king's room, that morning of the third of May.
They had pledged themselves to push the matter through that day, while the members opposed to reform were still away for the Easter
recess.

The excitement caused by the talk of a second partition was at its height. One of the
deputies called on the king to devise some
means to save the country.

In answer to this appeal Stanislas declared,
"It is my conviction that the only way to at-

tain safety is to establish a new constitution. The proposed plan for such a constitution I hold in my hands. I urge the members of the Diet to accept it. It is the last, it is the best way to save Poland."

The constitution was drafted in French, the work of king and patriot committee. It was modeled on the English constitution and on the one so recently made by the United States. But its details were adapted to the special needs of Poland.

Clause by clause the constitution was read, beginning with the famous words used on a similar occasion by the National Assembly of France:

"All power in a state emanates from the will of the nation."

Quietly the members of the Diet listened. Those who were not in the secret were astonished at the sweeping changes made in the government. They approved of abolishing the old, old veto which allowed one man to say "I forbid!" thus ending all discussion of a measure, ending too that session of the Diet. Yes, in public affairs a majority should rule.

The marshal read on. More and more changes—the townspeople to have a vote! the peasants to be under the law's protection! an established church for Poland, but no religious persecution for other faiths! a national army of one hundred thousand men, to be under the command of the king! Why, why, this meant doing away with the men-at-arms who for centuries had fought under the banners of their nobles. This meant an army now for Poland.

But most important of all was the paragraph declaring the crown hereditary. No longer elect their king by popular vote? The marshal was suddenly interrupted by a voice of protest. A man pushed his way toward the throne. Throwing himself at the king's feet he implored Stanislas to abandon this idea.

"It will be fatal to the liberty of Poland!" he cried.

"Nay, nay," cried several members, "it will end forever the uncertain, disturbed period between the death of a king and the choice of a new ruler. It is that that's been fatal to Poland!"

The patriots who had met in the king's room that morning now left their seats and rushed into the center of the hall.

"Swear, swear!" they loudly demanded. "Swear here and now!"

The bishop of Cracow was called to the throne. At his hands Stanislas took an oath on the gospels to defend the new constitution. The better to be seen by the members of the Diet and by the crowds in the gallery, he mounted on the seat and swore aloud.

With one accord the members held up their right hands and pledged themselves.

"I have sworn," said Stanislas with emotion, "and I will never swerve from it. Let every man that loves his country follow me to the cathedral of St. John, and thanking God let us repeat the oath at the altar."

"Long live the king! Long live the constitution!" answered the Diet.

What a procession that was from palace to cathedral! King and ministers, members of the Diet, bishops and visitors marched through the streets of Warsaw. Cheering and applauding, the crowds of people waiting outside the palace made way for them.

In their seats in the great hall sat twelve members who were opposed to reform. They were gloomily silent.

Before the high altar at St. John's, king and members recited the oath of loyalty. The *Te Deum* was sung. The noise of two hundred cannon greeted the announcement of the new constitution. The people's cries of joy filled the air. All night the streets of Warsaw were ablaze with illuminations.

Two days later the members of the Diet signed the new instrument of government. It made Poland a monarchy of the modern type, in an age when the rest of Europe had not begun to dream of a constitution. It was not perfect judged by our standards of today, but it was a long step in the right direction.

The Diet voted that this important event should be remembered and celebrated each year. Thus the third of May became the great holiday of Poland.

From almost every state in Europe congratulations poured in on Stanislas. This was indeed the triumph of his life. His ally, the king of Prussia, wrote a letter of well-wishing. The pope sent a message of congratulation. English statesmen who had deplored the French Revolution were enthusiastic in their admiration for Poland's new constitution, a model of its kind.

"It is a work," said Fox, "in which every friend to reasonable liberty must be sincerely interested."

And Burke exclaimed, "Humanity must rejoice and glory when it considers the change in Poland!"

In all the history of the world is there any revolution like this? It came without the shedding of one drop of blood. It came without the uprising of an oppressed class, overturning society to obtain its rights. Voluntarily the nobles of Poland voted to restrict their ancient privileges which dated back to the fourteenth century.

But no congratulations came from Catherine of Russia. Her alarm was the best proof of the excellence of the new constitution. Her consternation showed how much it promised of restored strength to Poland.

But alas! The third of May came too late to save the nation. The foreign relations committee had ample cause for fear. Poland's neighbors were powerful and ambitious. The last thing in the world they wanted was a reorganized Poland with a new constitution, with a large army, with a king who was no longer a figurehead.

While preparations were making in 1792 for a celebration on the third of May Russia declared war. On the nineteenth of the month the tramp of alien armies was heard on Polish soil. Eighty thousand Russian soldiers marched across the border. With them came twenty thousand Cossacks.

The constitution had provided for an army of one hundred thousand. But Poland had not had time or money to raise and equip that many soldiers. Against the Russians she could muster a bare twenty thousand.

Stanislas appealed to his ally Prussia. The answer was, "We agreed to help the Poland of the old constitution, not the new." She appealed to England and to France. But no help came. Her little army was defeated.

1793 saw the second partition of Poland carried through. Her territory was again taken by her neighbors, again four millions of her people. The treaty providing for this cession of land was read in the Diet. In gloomy silence the members listened. A vote was called for. Not one member responded.

"Silence gives consent," declared the marshal.

But the Poles proud of their past, of their noble traditions, refused tamely to accept these terms. Under the leadership of Kosciusko they formed the people's insurrection.

Bravely they fought with all the valor and courage of their ancestors.

Success was theirs—for a time. They delayed the Russian advance. They raised the siege of Warsaw. They drove out the foreign garrisons. Bit by bit they won back three-fourths of their ancient territory.

Then Russia moved more troops up from Turkey and hurled them against Poland. The king of Prussia came himself to lead his armies. In October of 1794 Kosciusko's little force was finally vanquished.

The following year saw the third and last partition of the country. Austria, Russia and Prussia each took a share. The names of the districts were altered. The laws of Poland were suspended. Another language was used.

The constitution of 1791, written on parchment, lay in a beautiful casket in the Kremlin palace at Moscow. From the map of Europe the word Poland was erased. So came to an end the history of the Polish republic.

But it was not the end of the Polish nation. The combined might of her three despoilers, even of all Europe could not kill this people that had such a passionate will to live. They were unconquerable.

They were a nation with a great and noble past through a thousand years of history. For centuries they had stood as the bulwark of Europe against the invasions of Turk and Mongol from the east. Persecuted and disowned after this third partition, their spiritual force grew not the less, but greater.

The third of May shall be celebrated each year to keep alive the memory of the new constitution, had been the decree of the Diet. For more than a century the day was celebrated, though often and often in secret. Fathers told its story to their children and pledged them anew in loyal service to Poland. Mothers told their sons and promised when they were old enough, they too should fight for Poland. From generation to generation they transmitted the watchword of protest against a foreign yoke.

At every change in Europe, in the wars of Napoleon, in the many struggles in which Austria and Russia and Prussia had a part, the Poles too fought. Now they were on this side, now on that, wherever there seemed a chance to fight for Poland. The name and fame of the Polish Legion was like that of their ancestors' regiment of hussars distinguished by the splendid wings of eagles' feathers, which on many a battlefield charged the foe and swept all before them.

Time after time the Poles rose in revolt against Russia. They were determined that some day there should be again a Poland on the map of Europe. This was their great dream, the vision which held them to their difficult task. It kept them loyal and patriotic in spite of persecution and sufferings.

In front of the Polish Museum at Rapperswill in Switzerland—for even their national museum was exiled—stands a great column bearing the dates of all these insurrections. Each generation has witnessed one or more. Always Poland waited for the favorable moment to regain her independence. Interrupted but not ended was her rôle in history. In the hearts of Poles their country never ceased to live. Her freedom was their one ideal.

After a hundred and twenty years of misfortune and defeat and disappointments the world war brought the opportunity for which Poland had been waiting. In the discussions following the armistice of November, 1918 she asked a hearing. In the shifting of boundaries made by the treaty of Versailles the country was recreated. On the new map of Europe Poland shows. She has a new constitution more democratic than that of 1791, just as it was more progressive than the constitution of any state in Europe of that day.

No longer is the third of May celebrated in secret. No longer is there any fear that the parades in Warsaw will be scattered by Cossacks with their terrible whips. No longer do Polish fathers pledge their sons to fight for Poland. Now young and old, they pledge themselves to serve her loyally and well.

Under the new flag of white and red, the flag of the new Poland, they celebrate the third of May.

IN THE CORNER OF A SOUTHERN CHURCHYARD

THE THIRTIETH OF MAY

"Oh, what lovely roses!"

"What beautiful lilacs you have! How fragrant they are!"

As they went toward the churchyard the little group of women exclaimed over the flowers they carried. But their thoughts were far away with the army of Virginia or with the troops defending Vicksburg. They thought too of the soldiers in gray who had given their lives at Shiloh and Corinth and Stone River. Not one of these southern women but had lost husband or son or brother in those desperate battles.

Two short years before they had seen the beginning of the war. There had been flags proudly waving, the rat-a-tat of drums, the silver bugles calling, the dauntless fife; then the parting and their men marching away under the stars and bars.

147

Since then there had been for the women of the South suffering and weary waiting; and for the men in gray long marches, battlefield and whirlwind charge, guard kept in wild storm or under the quiet stars, and for some of them hospital days and death.

On that April morning in 1863 this little group of women in Columbus, Mississippi went together to decorate the graves of their soldier dead. Roses, lilacs, lilies, all the flowers of that spring month they had gathered. Over the low mounds in the churchyard they strewed their blossoms, shedding tears in memory of their loved ones.

"Oh!" cried a woman of the group, "what are you doing?"

Having finished decorating the grave of her two sons an elderly lady was walking up the path toward a corner of the churchyard. Her arms were filled with lilacs and roses, red and white.

"Do you forget," the first woman cried, "whose graves those are? They're two Union soldiers. They're Yankees who—"

"Hush!" said the mother of the two heroes. "You are wrong. I do not forget. They are nameless graves marking where two soldiers lie buried. But somewhere in the North, in some city or little village or perhaps in some lonely farmhouse, a mother or a young wife or sweetheart mourns for them just as you and I grieve for our dead."

She turned back to the unmarked graves and stooped down. Gently she pushed aside the long grass. Tenderly she spread her flowers over the two mounds. With tears in her eyes, but with her head held proudly she faced the women who had silently gathered about her.

"We bring these flowers," she pointed to the grave of her sons, then to others decked with blossoms, "to express our love and devotion. They are dead, our heroes of the South. They are dead, these unknown soldiers of the North, lying here in our churchyard in Columbus in nameless graves. But when the war is over and peace comes again we shall call them all heroes. So here are my lilacs and my roses, red and white and blue, for both alike."

"And mine."

"And mine."

"And mine too," said the other women

softly as they added their flowers to the lovely blossoms on the unmarked graves in the corner.

The next April and the next the women of Columbus repeated this beautiful deed though with each year their privations and suffering were greater, the losses of the South more irreparable. More and more graves filled the churchyard, graves of brave Southerners who fell at Vicksburg and Chancellorsville, at Gettysburg and in the Wilderness; graves of brave Northerners who died in the South fighting for the Union.

More and more women joined the group that went each spring to decorate the graves of soldiers who had worn the gray, who had worn the blue. With their flowers they covered all the mounds in the churchyard as impartially as the sunshine falls upon the just and the unjust.

A little thing perhaps—to strew blossoms on a grave. But from this act of the women of Columbus came the most beautiful of our holidays.

When the fighting had been over for two years, but while there were still great bitterness and resentment in many hearts both

North and South, the New York *Tribune*
printed a brief dispatch telling the story of
these southern women. In towns and villages
all through the northern states that paragraph
was republished. The people were thrilled
with tenderness. Their hearts were touched.
As nothing else could have done, those few
sentences called out friendship and love to re-
place sectional hatred and passion.

"Flowers for the graves of northern and
southern soldiers alike—for the blue and for
the gray!" exclaimed the North. "Peace has
come indeed. We are not enemies, but
friends. With malice toward none, with
charity for all—and it is the bereaved, suffering women of the South who set us the example. We are brothers again, not foes. No
longer a North and a South, but the Union.
And Union means peace and harmony and
good will."

Early in May of 1868 it was suggested to
General John A. Logan, then national commander of the G. A. R., that their organiza-
tion borrow this beautiful custom and have a
uniform day for decorating the graves of their
fallen comrades. Logan issued an order nam-
ing the thirtieth of May, choosing this date be-

cause it marked the discharge of the last soldier in the Union army.

Touched by the story of the Mississippi women and the beauty of their custom, state after state in the North declared this day a holiday. In some of the southern states May tenth is observed. Louisiana has the third of June. In four states it is April twenty-sixth.

Throughout the South, throughout the North, not a city or town or village but sent its men to the war, dressed in blue or dressed in gray. To some of those homes, North and South, soldiers came not back when the war was ended. So North and South alike honor them with the coming of each springtime.

As nature covers over scars of battle and decorates with her living green, so the strewing of flowers on the graves of our soldiers has been an effective agent in healing over the wounds of civil war. The suffering, the terror, the losses of the war North and South alike regret. But in that struggle the nation was remade. Fighting, falling, dying were the steps toward the future when we should be indeed one nation, united and inseparable.

Not holidays, but holy days are these memorial days when North and South pause in the busy work of the modern world and pay tribute to the heroes in blue and in gray who lost their lives that the Union might endure. Nor do we remember only the soldiers of the civil war.   In 1899 the veterans of the Spanish war began decorating the graves of their comrades.   In May of 1919 men who had fought in France and in the fields of Flanders paid tribute to their soldier dead.   Peasant women and children of France living near the battle front gathered flowers to lay on the graves of American soldiers who had died overseas.

"We do this," they explained simply, "not as strangers, but for their mothers who are far away."

Lilacs, roses red and white, the poppies that grow in Flanders fields, wild flowers from the roadside—all serve for our memorial days. With love and tears we pay this honor to our soldiers.   And in the doing we rekindle our own patriotism and dedicate ourselves anew to the nation for which they sacrificed their lives.

"WE MUST ALL HANG TOGETHER"

THE FOURTH OF JULY

In the city of Philadelphia that eighth of July in the year 1776 there was eager discussion. Everywhere was an undercurrent of excitement. It seemed to center around the red brick State House.

People began to gather—men and women, a few children. More and more came until there was a crowd in the yard, standing close up around the platform that had been built for quite another purpose—built seven years before by a scientific society for astronomical observations.

In the air was a tense, overwrought feeling that increased as time passed and noon came nearer. The crowd in the State House yard was very grave. This was a solemn occasion. However things ended this was a crisis in the affairs of the colonies.

Thoughtful men in that Quaker city had watched for years the ebb and flow of a tide

154

in the relations of England to her settlements in the new world. The closing of the port of Boston, the sending of British troops and quartering them on the people, the orders to arrest Hancock and Adams, the expedition to Lexington and Concord—these had been successive stages of the tide.

Slow but never stopping, of late it had been coming with a rush and a roar. When fighting began at the green in Lexington and at the Concord bridge there was scarcely a man in all America who talked of independence. They were Englishmen asking, demanding from Parliament and king their rights as loyal subjects of George III. But now, as when each fresh wave rolls in with ever rising strength, now the sentiment in favor of independence had been growing stronger and stronger.

So a tall, grave sailor talked with two friends in the crowd that Monday morning in July.

"You're wrong to say the tide," interposed his companion. "That comes and goes each day, nay, twice a day. This is something deeper, stronger, more important in every way. Why don't you compare it to a glacier whose movement may be slow at first, but increases as it moves down the mountain side? This didn't begin a year ago last April. Why, man, you want to go back at least eleven years, back to the stamp act and Patrick Henry's speech, back to the war with the French and the question of how its debts were to be paid."

"Aye, he's right there," said the third man. "And thou art right too when thou sayest nobody, or maybe a dozen men in all these thirteen colonies, thought of independence a year ago. Today it's on every man's tongue. 'Tis the king himself who's driven us to it. Injustice has killed our affection for him. Proof that the people have been thinking it over? Look at the crowd out this Monday noon when the sheriff is to read the new declaration that Congress voted for last Thursday."

"It was that young lawyer from Virginia said we raised our army with no idea of separation from the mother country. And now," commented the sailor with a smile, "they say he's the very man who wrote this declaration of independence."

"Aye, but that was a year ago. Think of what's happened since—the royal governors driven out of Virginia and North Carolina,

Norfolk bombarded, Portland burned, Canada invaded, the British forced to give up Boston, the Hessians hired to fight us."

"What a catalogue you roll up! Isn't it almost a farce when we've been fighting for more than a year, to keep on talking of ourselves as loyal Englishmen instead of independent Americans?"

"Thou'rt quoting Tom Paine and his famous pamphlet, *Common Sense*. A man must agree with much he says. But it's so grave a business, friend. Our hands once put to the plough there's no turning back."

"Look, there comes the committee of safety."

There was more than one straw showing that the wind of public opinion was pointing in a new direction. As early as May of '75 a county in North Carolina had adopted resolutions touching on independence and sent them to their delegates in the Continental Congress at Philadelphia. But they thought the time not yet ripe to lay the suggestion before that body.

Waiting a year North Carolina instructed her representatives to concur with other members of Congress in a declaration of independence. In May Virginia went a step farther and told her delegates to propose such a declaration. Georgia and Rhode Island and South Carolina expressed a willingness to agree to any measures which Congress thought would promote the general welfare. All during May town meetings in Massachusetts put themselves on record in favor of independence.

A year ago that very month Massachusetts had framed a government for herself, which in no way recognized the king of England. New Hampshire had followed her example, then South Carolina. In May Congress advised the other colonies to form new governments, changing themselves into states because George III had withdrawn his protection. Wasn't that almost a declaration of independence? After hot debate and earnest opposition from the middle colonies Congress voted for this measure.

That May was an interesting month in Philadelphia, and June more so. On Friday the seventh, obeying the instructions of his colony of Virginia, Richard Henry Lee, the oldest member of the delegation, rose and read to Congress a resolution "that these United Colonies are, and of right ought to be, free and independent States; that they are absolved from

all allegiance to the British Crown; and that
all political connection between them and the
State of Great Britain is, and ought to be, to-
tally dissolved." The next paragraph proposed that a plan of confederation be prepared
and sent to the colonies for consideration. Independence and union hand in hand!

Quickly John Adams of Massachusetts sec-
onded the proposal. The debate began at
once and continued on Saturday and Monday.
Two men from Pennsylvania and Livingston
of New York led the opposition. The people
of the middle colonies, they said, were not
ready to break off relations with the mother
country.

"The Tories are stronger in New York than
elsewhere," they urged. "Our grievances are
fewer. We have more to risk than any other
colony—invasion from Canada, an attack by
the powerful British fleet, on the west the terrible Iroquois, at every point we are exposed.
Indeed we're not less patriotic than other
places. But wait—perhaps a change of ministers in England will adjust all our difficulties."

Pushed to the wall they acknowledged that
lingering hopes of settling the trouble were a

dream and a delusion.   Yet they hesitated to
take the final step.

"The middle colonies," commented Jefferson comparing them to fruit in an orchard,
"are not yet matured for falling from the par-
ent stem, but fast advancing to that state."

It was highly important that all the colonies
think together and work together. If the van-
guard was marching too fast the laggards must
be given time to catch up.   Further discussion
was postponed until the first day of July.   By
that time Congress could hear from those colonies which had not yet declared themselves.

But they must guard against losing time
when the resolution was taken up again.   A
committee was named to prepare a declaration
of independence, to be ready when wanted.
Its members were chosen by vote: Thomas
Jefferson of Virginia, John Adams, Dr.
Franklin, Roger Sherman of Connecticut and
Robert R. Livingston of New York—three
lawyers, a printer and a shoemaker.   Richard
Henry Lee was absent, suddenly called to Virginia by the illness of his wife.

The committee met and with one voice the
four members urged that Jefferson write the
declaration stating the reasons for the war and

for separation from England. He was only thirty-two, but they all knew why he had been chosen, with more votes than any of them. He was no orator, but a brilliant writer. He had a ready and eloquent pen. America called upon him now to use it. And there was another motive. Jefferson had no enemies. He had taken no share in the debates in Congress. There would be no risk of any interference from personal feelings. Therefore the members had put him first on the committee. The natural result was that he did the bulk of its work.

In a new brick house at what is now the corner of Market and Seventh Streets, but was then out in the fields Jefferson had rented a furnished parlor and bedroom on the second floor. In that parlor, writing on a little desk three inches high, he spent three weeks on a first draft.

He was the mouthpiece of America. Without using books or pamphlets he wrote out in clear, plain paragraphs what the people had been thinking and saying. Here and there he changed phrases. He hunted for just the right word to express his meaning and not give undue offense. Frequently he stopped to take up his beloved violin and play. In time of work and stress it never failed to divert him.

Before the end of June he showed his paper to Franklin and to Adams separately. He asked for corrections. Only two or three they were; you can see them, interlined in their handwritings, in the original draft in the Department of State in Washington.

Then the committee was called together. The report with the suggestions of Adams and Franklin embodied in it was adopted. Jefferson wrote out a fresh copy.

Quickly June passed into July. On Monday the first the fifty members of Congress declared themselves a committee of the whole and took up the Lee resolution. There was more debate and a vote was called for. Now in the Continental Congress members voted not as individuals, but as colonies. Three to two, or six to five, or eight to one, the majority of votes in each delegation determined the vote of that colony, yes or no, for or against any motion. A two-thirds vote was necessary to carry, nine out of thirteen.

On the Lee resolution nine voted yes. No, said Pennsylvania and South Carolina. Delaware could not vote: she had three delegates, one said yes, one no, the third was absent on a trip through the lower counties of his state arguing against the loyalists. New York too did not vote.

"We are in favor of the resolution," explained her delegates, "and believe our citizens are. But we're still under instructions drawn up a year ago which strictly forbid us to take any action against reconciliation with England."

This was however a preliminary ballot. At the request of South Carolina the final vote was postponed till the next day. Then the result was quite different: after a night ride of eighty miles the missing Delaware man arrived and voted yes; Pennsylvania changed her vote because two members opposed to the resolution stayed away; South Carolina now said yes, that the records might show Congress unanimously in favor of independence. Again New York cast no vote, but a few days later the state convention sent its approval of the Lee resolution.

The Rubicon was crossed. The thirteen English colonies had become the United States of America. It was a bold step they were taking. For the sake of safety Congress directed the secretary to omit from the journal the names of Lee and Adams as mover and seconder of the resolution.

Later that day the delegates took up the committee's report on the declaration of independence. The debate began. It lasted for hours, all the next day and till a late hour on Thursday, the fourth. It seemed indeed as though discussion would go on endlessly. Perhaps it might have at any other time of the year.

The weather was very hot. Close by the State House was a stable from which horse-flies swarmed, thick and fierce. They lit on the legs of the delegates and bit through their thin silk stockings.

"Better treason than to be so uncomfortable," whispered one member to another. "Let's call for a vote to escape these flies."

Treason? Yes, every man there knew how important was the step they were taking. Once adopt this report of the committee, once declare their independence of England, and there was no going back. To the mother country they were bound by many ties—ties of blood and speech, of daily life and intercourse, of thought and business. They had the same ideals, the same hopes, the same beliefs.

Separate themselves from England? That meant war to the bitter end. The king's armies were still in the land. Not always were the colonists victorious. George III had money and men without limit and credit everywhere. The Americans had no funds and no credit. A straggling chain of settlements clinging to the seaboard, they were defying the greatest power in the world.

If they won, well and good. If they lost, the hangman's rope for traitors. For the leaders in civil and military circles this was a choice of independence or ruin with no middle ground.

It was a dangerous step they were considering and was so regarded in London. Lee's son was there at school. One day a visitor asked, "Who is that?"

"The son of Richard Henry Lee of America."

"Ah." The man turned to the lad. "We shall yet see your father's head upon Tower Hill."

"You may have it when you can get it," replied young Lee.

For three days the members discussed Jefferson's draft for their declaration of independence. Some changes they made for greater accuracy of statement. One paragraph they voted to omit entirely—the one denouncing George III for encouraging the slave trade. True, he had done all that Jefferson said. But was it wise to denounce the king when this trade was carried on by northern shipowners for southern purchasers?

A second passage Congress omitted, a statement that the hiring of foreign troops by the English must "cause us to endeavor to forget our former love for them." Better not say a word that could be construed as a reflection on the English people. Our quarrel is with George III, not with the people of England.

During all this discussion Thomas Jefferson spoke not once. Perhaps this was because he did not feel able to hold his own in so strenuous a contest of oratory. Perhaps he thought it his duty to be a passive listener to the comments of impartial judges. But he was far from cheerful while sharp criticisms were being made.

Benjamin Franklin sitting by him saw the young Virginian writhe more than once under some bitter speech. By way of comfort he said, "You know, Jefferson, the story of John Thompson the hatter?"

The author of the declaration shook his head.

"He was one of my apprentice friends who was going to open shop for himself. He ordered a handsome signboard with the inscription, *John Thompson, Hatter, makes and sells hats for ready money,* with the figure of a hat. He submitted it to some friends for their amendments. The first thought the word *Hatter* unnecessary. It was struck out. The next said *makes* might as well be omitted, because customers didn't care who made the hats. It was painted over. A third observed *for ready money* was useless, as it wasn't the custom to sell on credit. *'Sells?'* said the next friend, 'why, nobody expects you to give them away.' *Sells* was left out. 'Why *hats,* when there's one painted on the board?' asked another. So the inscription was reduced to *John Thompson* with the picture of a hat."

Wisely Jefferson kept out of the debate. The burden of upholding the committee fell to John Adams. So gallantly he bore it that the author said afterward, "He was our Colossus on the floor."

Congress adopted the committee's declaration of independence. John Hancock as president and Thomson as secretary of Congress signed it, Hancock making his large, familiar signature that reached across the page and saying jestingly, "There! John Bull can read that without spectacles. Now let him double the price on my head, for this is my defiance." Then he became serious and impressed on his fellow-delegates the necessity of their standing together in this matter. "Gentlemen, we must all hang together. We must be unanimous. There must be no pulling different ways."

"Yes," said Franklin with his quaint, dry humor, "we must all hang together or most assuredly we shall all hang separately."

"When it comes to the hanging," said big, bluff Harrison from Virginia to the meager, little Gerry of Massachusetts, "I shall have the advantage of you. It'll all be over with me before you've done kicking in the air."

The hangman's rope for traitors to England was never far from their minds. The business of Congress went on. It was voted that the committee which had prepared it should superintend and correct the printing of the declaration; that copies should be sent to all commit-

tees of safety, to army officers, to all the states;
that it should be proclaimed in each state and
at the head of the army. Congress ordered
further that at noon on the eighth of July at
the State House in Philadelphia the sheriff
should read it in public, and that the members
of the committee of safety should meet at their
chamber and proceed in a body to the State
House.

But of all these details the good people of
Philadelphia knew little or nothing. Sessions
of Congress were in secret behind closed doors.
Not till after the fourth had come and gone did
the citizens learn that Thursday was the birthday of a new nation. On the sixth a Philadelphia newspaper printed the declaration.

Word had spread abroad of what was to
happen on the eighth. The sailor and his
friends with a great crowd of people watched
the committee of safety take their places.
Colonel John Nixon, it was announced, would
read the declaration of independence. The
sheriff had invited him to do this, perhaps because he was in charge of the city's defense,
perhaps because he had a fine, far-carrying
voice.

The people were very quiet. Slowly, distinctly, impressively the colonel began: "When in the course of human events—" Men were leaning forward to hear the better. "We hold these truths to be self-evident, that all men are created equal, that they are endowed—" Then followed the announcement of political rights applying to all mankind. "Let facts be submitted to a candid world."

Sentence by sentence Nixon read the twenty-seven grievances of the colonies which justified the Revolution. The crowd in the yard was hushed. They realized the tremendous importance of this step. Impressively, but with a voice no longer steady the colonel came to the closing paragraph, the ringing, fearless statement that the colonies were free and independent states and that for the support of this declaration the delegates pledged their lives, their fortunes and their sacred honor.

Applause followed the reading and a murmur of heartfelt satisfaction. The bell in the wooden steeple of the State House began to ring, the bell from London which bore those marvelous words from the Bible, "Proclaim liberty throughout all the land, unto all the inhabitants thereof."

The following day Washington ordered the declaration read to every brigade of the army in New York City. Near where the City Hall now stands the troops paraded and listened while their officers read Jefferson's paper. The soldiers greeted it with loud cheers. That night the gilded lead statue of George III in Bowling Green was pulled down and melted to make bullets to be fired against the king's men.

Meanwhile swift couriers had been sent out from Philadelphia carrying copies of the declaration from the press of John Dunlop. From town to town, from colony to colony they spread the news. Everywhere from New Hampshire down to Georgia the people rejoiced at the glad tidings. There were banquets and bonfires, illumination of houses, firing of cannon, flying of flags.

Nothing up to that time had brought the colonists so close together, rallying the thirteen peoples into one earnest body of patriots. They had announced to the world their independence. Together they would fight till it was won, till the English king and Parliament acknowledged this new nation across the Atlantic.

A fine copy of the declaration was made, engrossed on parchment. On the second of August it was brought into Congress for the members to sign. Again Hancock wrote his name in the same large letters. Again there was joking among the members to hide their serious thoughts. Were they signing warrants for their own execution?

"You're safe," some one said when Charles Carroll signed, "for there are so many Carrolls in Maryland the king will never know where to find you."

"I'll show him," was the answer and Carroll wrote "of Carrollton" after his name.

Because of this delay of nearly a month the parchment copy with the signatures of the delegates, the copy preserved in Washington, does not represent exactly the Congress that met on the fourth of July. All who voted for it did not sign it. Some signed in August who were not members a month earlier.

May thirty-first, 1775, when a Carolina county took the first step looking toward independence; June seventh when Lee introduced his resolution; the second of July when it was voted on; July the fourth when Jefferson's declaration of independence was adopted; the

second of August when it was formally signed
—which is the birthday of the nation?

Adams said the credit was Richard Henry
Lee's and the second of July would be remembered always and celebrated as a day of deliverance from one end of the country to the
other. But by common consent the people of
America settled on the fourth of July. It has
been known ever since as the birthday of the
republic, founded on principles of liberty and
justice.

With speeches and ringing of bells, with
firing of cannon and flying of flags, with an im-
pressive public reading of the declaration of
independence we keep this holiday in all the
states of the Union, now grown from thirteen
to forty-eight, much as the news was celebrated
in 1776. With each year deeper grows our
love of independence and our gratitude to
those members of the Continental Congress
who hung together lest they should hang separately.

AN EMPEROR'S SAFE-CONDUCT

This is a holiday in Czechoslovakia. Everywhere flags are flying, flags of white and red
with a blue triangle. There are flags flying
in Prague, at the university, at the old bridge,
and in Bethlehem Square where once stood the
famous chapel. There are flags out today in
the village of Husinec near the Bavarian frontier. In every part of Czechoslovakia people
stop their work to pay tribute to the greatest
Czech in history.

Miles away in Switzerland, in the city of
Constance visitors are making a pilgrimage to
the tablet-marked house at 66 Husenstrasse,
and to the Merchants' Exchange where the
great council met, and to the cathedral to seek
out the stone slab in the nave, twelve paces
from the entrance, where more than five centuries ago, on this very sixth of July, a man
stood to receive sentence. They drive out to
the Brühl, a beautiful meadow half a mile be-

yond the city walls, and lay their flowers on an ivy-covered boulder.

Since that long ago sixth of July in 1415 Bohemians have kept this day. But notice! Many of the flags in Prague and Husinec are at half mast.

This is not an ordinary holiday. It celebrates not a great victory, a happy birthday, or some event that helped to make Bohemia free. It is not famous for a king or for a general or for a statesman. Yet it is kept by all Bohemia—rich and poor, old and young, Protestant and Catholic, peasant and noble.

It is Jan Hus day.

Not a general? Not a ruler? Not a statesman? No, Hus was a preacher. Who would have prophesied a great future for him when in 1389 fatherless and poor he left his home in the village of Husinec to go up to the university of Prague? So poor he was, all he had to offer to the rector for his admission as a student was a goose, with a cake his mother had baked. But on the journey, says the old legend, the goose flew away. So the rector received only the cake. So poor he was that he sang on the street and in churches to earn a few pennies.

Yet Jan Hus made himself a scholar and a leader. He was in turn student, bachelor of arts, then master. He lectured, served as dean of one of the faculties, and was finally rector of the university. In 1400 he was ordained a priest.

Two years later he became the preacher at the Bethlehem Chapel. A large church that must have been, for it seated a thousand persons. Two rich merchants had built and endowed it with the condition that its sermons must be in the Bohemian tongue. People of all classes thronged to hear Hus preach. His pulpit was like a throne. His influence was as great, sometimes greater than king's or archbishop's.

Fearless he was in all he preached. Over and over he denounced the idle rich for their misdeeds, denounced the clergy for selling church offices, for their worldliness and greed. Like the challenge of a John the Baptist his fearless words rang out. Men who felt themselves accused resolved to silence this preacher who praised poverty and virtue and self-sacrifice.

Many enemies he had—parish priests who were envious of his popularity; the foreign professors in the university, for Hus was a devoted patriot and the champion of Bohemia; the higher clergy and prelates of the church whose lives he condemned; and the monks whose wealth he disapproved.

But he had also many friends—the common people who flocked to the chapel in Bethlehem Square because of his marvelous eloquence and his piety; many of the nobles at court; Queen Sophia whose confessor he was; and for some time the king.

One day a nobleman complained at court that Jan Hus was attacking the idle rich for their besetting sins. The king summoned the archbishop and told him to warn this fiery preacher to be more cautious in his language.

"No, your Majesty," replied the archbishop, "no. Hus is bound by his ordination oath to speak the truth without respect of persons."

The king must perforce agree. Presently the attacks were turned from nobles to clergy. Again there was complaint at court.

"Your Majesty," the archbishop urged, "this fiery preacher must be warned to be more cautious in his language. His words are too rash. They do more harm than good."

"No," replied the king, "no. Hus is bound

by his oath to speak the truth without respect of persons."

Only a few years before Wycliffe had been teaching in England some of the doctrines Jan Hus taught in Bohemia. Did he learn of Wycliffe's books through the king's sister, the bride of Richard II of England? or through some English students, graduates of Oxford, who came to Prague?

The university declared forty-five articles quoted from Wycliffe's writings to be heresy. Hus protested, but in vain. The archbishop of Prague demanded that all copies of these books be given to him. In the courtyard of his palace two hundred of them were burned while the church bells tolled and the priests chanted.

Now at that time books were few and costly. Parchment was precious. Scribes penned the letters by hand with long hours of labor. The king ordered the full value of the burned books to be paid to the owners. Humiliated and embarrassed, the archbishop who till now had been a friend of Jan Hus became angry with him. Publicly he was excommunicated amid the indignant shouts of the people.

In the Bethlehem Chapel this fearless

preacher continued to speak—to thousands. His listeners overflowed into the streets.

In 1412 two men arrived at Prague. Drummers went before them to attract people's attention. In the market place they established themselves. To all the passersby they called out to enlist as soldiers in a crusade the pope had declared against the king of Naples. In return they would receive pardon for their sins. Those who could not fight must give money or goods and they too would receive indulgences.

Here was another chance for Hus to denounce the greed of the church. Like Martin Luther a century later he posted on the chapel doors a thesis denouncing this unholy traffic. From the Bethlehem pulpit he thundered against it.

He brought the matter before the university. There was a stormy debate in the great hall. Hus argued against the sale of indulgences. He drew his material chiefly from the writings of Wycliffe. The practise was declared unchristian. The papal bull was burned.

In reply the pope excommunicated Jan Hus. He was declared cut off from "food, drink, buying and selling, from conversation and hospitality, from the giving of fire and water and all other acts of kindness." All true members of the church were forbidden to have any intercourse with him. All religious services were to be suspended in any town he entered.

The answer of Hus was, "I appeal from the pope to Christ."

The whole city of Prague was laid under the interdict. The churches were closed. Hoping to end the conflict the king asked Hus to retire for a time. Down to his birthplace at Husinec went the preacher, "not," said he, "to deny the truth for which I am willing to die, but because the church forbids the preaching of it."

Here for twenty months he preached—in the villages, in castles, in fields and forests, in public squares, wherever men would hear him. Through the entire land his doctrines were spreading. Everywhere he was gaining friends and followers.

It was during these months of voluntary exile that Hus did the most of his literary work. Fifteen books in Bohemian he wrote and several in Latin. He revised the Bohemian translation of the Bible, made in the previous cen-

tury. He wrote many hymns. Jealous for
the language of his people he devised a new
system of spelling, made rules for the many
different dialects, and purified it from German
words. How much the tongue of Bohemia
owes to the preacher of Bethlehem Chapel!

When in October of 1414 he returned to
Prague Hus was as popular and as fearless as
before. It was a time of alarms and unrest
and confusion. How could there be peace in
the university or in the city or in the kingdom?

For this preacher, said his enemies, was a
dangerous reformer, a violent agitator. He
taught doctrines that had been condemned.
And he taught them with a flaming eloquence
that carried all before it.

A great council was to be held in Switzerland to make some reforms in the Catholic
church. Sigismund, the emperor of Germany,
summoned Hus to appear before this council
of Constance. He promised such ample protection for the journey that "he should come
unmolested to Constance, there have free right
of audience and, should he not submit to the
decision of the Council, he should return un-
harmed."

Three Bohemian nobles were appointed to

accompany Hus and assist him on the road. On the eleventh of October the group set forth though many of his friends begged Hus not to go.

"You will never return to Prague," they prophesied sadly.

"I must go," was his answer. "This is my opportunity to vindicate my position. I must prove that I believe and teach nothing contrary to the accepted faith of the church."

The party arrived at Constance early in November. In a little house near the Schnetz gate Hus took up his lodging.

Not many days had passed when he had a visit from three men who requested him to come to the pope's palace for a conference with the cardinals. The place was surrounded by soldiers. He had no choice but to go. The good woman of the house took leave of him with tears, fearing she would never see him again.

"But I have the emperor's safe-conduct!" said Hus.

He lifted his hands to bless her and rode away.

The cardinals asked a few questions.

"I am come," was his reply, "to make my defense in open meeting, after the arrival of the emperor under whose safe-conduct I am here."

Of this his accusers took no heed. They sent him to prison, not to the ordinary jail, but to the dungeon of an old monastery on a little island in the lake of Constance—the same building that is today an hotel. Without books or papers, without a Bible he was left there alone. Such a miserable, underground cell it was that he became very ill.

"It would never do to let him die!" exclaimed his enemies.

The pope sent his own physician to treat this Bohemian preacher. Hus was moved to a convent where he was fettered day and night. Like Paul in heavy chains he wrote letters to his friends.

Not until Christmas Eve did the emperor Sigismund arrive at Constance. Immediately a group of Bohemian lords complained to him of the imprisonment of Hus. He promised to use his influence to secure the preacher's freedom.

Now Sigismund had given this man his safe-conduct. He knew that any violent measure would result in trouble in Bohemia, perhaps even in revolution. But his sympathies were

all on the side of the church. He made only a
feeble protest. The council ignored it.

Days and weeks and months dragged by.
In March of 1415 the pope left Constance secretly. Hus then became the prisoner of the
emperor who had full power to set him free.
But Sigismund was afraid of the church. He
did nothing.

The friends of Hus were finally allowed to
visit him in his cell. They found him stretched
on a wretched couch. He was wasted almost
to a skeleton. He had been scantily fed from
the pope's table. Since his flight the prisoner
had been starving. With streaming eyes the
Bohemians lifted their hands to heaven and
prayed for an opportunity to avenge this cruel
wrong with their swords.

Again they protested to Sigismund. The
following day Hus was placed in charge of the
bishop of Constance who imprisoned him in
the tower of his castle. Here too he was kept
in chains. During the day he could move
about the room. At night his arm was chained
to the wall. Over two months he spent here
seeing no one, not allowed even to have letters.

After the pope's case was finished, on the
fifth of June the council took up the charges

against Jan Hus. He asked for a lawyer to advise him.

"A heretic," they answered him, "is not entitled to counsel."

"Well, then," said Hus, "let Jesus be my advocate."

From that moment he knew that he was already condemned. But he continued the fight not for life, but for the truth.

At his first sentence of defense a furious storm of contradiction and denunciation broke out. It was impossible for him to answer.

"I thought," he commented, "this council would be conducted in a manner more seemly."

The trial broke up in confusion and was continued on the seventh and eighth of the month. The churchmen asked a running fire of questions. They hurled at Hus all the acts and utterances of his life—what he had taught, what he had preached, his appeal from the pope to Christ, his quotations from Wycliffe, paragraphs from his books away from their context.

Many of the charges he denied. Some he admitted and wished to argue saying, "I will gladly change my beliefs if any one can show me they are not true."

But this the council would not permit.

"Don't argue. Say yes or no," they insisted. "You must retract *all* the heretical doctrines attributed to you and promise not to preach them again."

"I refuse," said Jan Hus boldly. "I'd rather die than retract with my lips opinions held in my heart."

Back to prison they led him. As he passed out through the crowd one man came up and grasped him by the hand. It was a daring thing to do and dangerous. Deeply it touched the lonely prisoner's heart.

The weather was stifling. People fled to the mountains to escape the heat. But for a month Hus remained in his cramped cell.

Daily his enemies argued with him trying to force him to recant, to acknowledge the errors of which he was accused. His reply was always the same.

"God is my witness that I have never taught or preached those things which have falsely been ascribed to me. The chief aim of my preaching, writing and acts has been that I might save men from sin. Today I am willing and glad to die for the truth which I have taught, written and preached."

The council refused any further hearing. For thirty weary days of heat and exhaustion this nagging went on. On the fifth of July came a last group of the clergy to induce him to recant. Steadfast he continued.

"I can not offend God," he declared, "by saying I held to heresies I never held. Abjure what I never taught? Be false to my conscience? Better to die than tell an untruth!"

"If the council," argued one of his visitors, "should say you have but one eye, Jan Hus, you are bound to agree that it is so."

"Nay, nay! If the whole world tells me I have but one eye I can not, so long as I have reason, say so without doing violence to my conscience!"

The next morning they brought him to the cathedral. All the notables of church and state were present. Mass was said. Hus was considered unworthy to enter and forced to wait outside. When the service was over he was led to a platform in the nave—the spot where today you see a white stone in the pavement.

An official read the charges against him.

"Not guilty!" said Jan Hus. He turned directly toward Sigismund. "I came here freely to this council relying on the public faith of the emperor who is here present, assuring me that I should be safe from all violence."

Under his steady gaze the emperor's face crimsoned.

A century later at Worms men urged Charles V to seize Martin Luther.

"No," was the reply, "he has a safe-conduct. I should not like to blush like Sigismund."

"For a last time we call upon you to recant," said the clerk of the council.

Hus refused.

"Then we declare you a heretic."

They read the condemnation with the charges. Over and over the prisoner broke in denying the truth of the accusations. Once when they read an entirely new charge he shrieked aloud and called out, "Give me the name of this accuser."

"Be silent."

Hus knelt down on the platform and prayed.

"Lord Jesus, pardon all my enemies for thy great mercy. Thou knowest that they have falsely accused me. Pardon them for thy mercy's sake."

The clergy and the people gathered around received these words with shouts of laughter.

They clothed him in white as a priest celebrating mass. Then they stripped from him the insignia of his ministry. They cut his hair to hide the tonsure. They snatched the chalice from his hands. They degraded him from his office and expelled him from the church.

Sigismund turned to the Count Palatine, the sword-bearer of the empire.

"Go, take him!"

For by the barbarous laws of that time the punishment for a heretic was death by burning. It was meted out not by the church, but by the civil authorities.

On the prisoner's head they put a paper cap, with a writing on it that he was a heretic, and a picture of three grinning devils clawing at his soul.

"The crown that Jesus wore was heavier and more painful than this," was his only comment.

The long procession slowly made its way from the cathedral to the city walls. There were eight hundred men-at-arms guarding a preacher with his hands bound. There were priests and prelates of the church. There were friends of the condemned from Prague. There were throngs of people. There were curious ones come to see a brave man die.

Out at the Schnetz gate they went, and half a mile beyond the walls of Constance to the meadow called the Brühl. They passed a place where the writings of Hus were being burned. The author smiled.

The crowd scattered into a wide circle around the stake. Great piles of fagots were ready near it. A chain about his neck, Jan Hus was bound to the stake. Straw and wood were heaped about him breast high. By chance his face was toward the east.

"Turn him the other way, the heretic!" cried the mob.

The executioner turned him to the west, the region of sunset and night.

"We commit thy soul to the devil!" thundered his enemies in chorus.

"And I," Jan Hus answered, "commit it to the most gracious Lord Jesus."

The fagots were lighted. The flames shot upward. Hus prayed aloud. Above the crackling of the fire the people could hear his voice, fearless as of old. The words were the opening sentence of the apostles' creed.

In the eyes of Hus was a rare light of joy. A strong gust of wind blew the smoke into his face.

"A breeze in this quiet weather?" cried some of the mob. "A miracle! A miracle!"

The words of the prisoner ceased. His lips still moved in prayer. The flames suffocated him.

"We know not his fault," said the spectators sympathetically, "but he prays like a true man of God."

The ashes from his body and from the fagots, even the pieces of the stake itself were thrown into the river Rhine, lest his friends carry them back to Prague as precious relics. His memory and example the fires of Constance could not burn.

All Bohemia mourned when the tidings came from Switzerland. It was the beginning, not the end of discord in the land. The people rose to avenge the death of their hero. Promptly war broke out, the devastating Hussite wars that lasted for fifty years.

Hus gave his life for the truth, saying it was better to die well than to live badly. He was the first man in history to stand for truth against the world, for freedom to think, to speak, to worship.

Since that long ago 1415 Bohemia has kept his day. She holds dearest the story of this brave Czech. Protestant and Catholic alike recognize his patriotism, his greatness of soul. And on the five hundredth anniversary of his death they united to honor their hero and martyr, the saint of his age, with a statue in Prague.

TWENTY MINUTES OF SIX

THE FOURTEENTH OF JULY

Today the tricolor is flying in France. In every little village, at every Hôtel de Ville flutters the red, white and blue. Every town is having fireworks and dancing. You can feel the holiday spirit in the air.

Especially is this true in the city of Paris. Wherever you look the tricolor is fluttering against the sky. All the shops are closed and tightly shuttered, but over their doors wave the flags of France.

Along the boulevards men and women and children walk gaily. The little boats that ply up and down the Seine have more passengers than they can take. The railroad stations are crowded. All Paris is leaving town to spend the day in the country. A still larger throng waits on the quay by the Louvre where the motor-bus starts for the twelve-mile drive to Versailles.

Here comes the mother with little Yvonne,

the father carrying the big basket of lunch, Lucien and Jacques minus their black sateen aprons, and twelve-year-old Renée. In France the family always celebrates a holiday together. Up they clamber to the top of the bus.

"How warm the sun is!" calls out Jacques. "Think how lovely it will be in the park at Versailles! You're sure, Mother, the fountains will play today? Will they be as wonderful as Renée says—great jets of water seventy-five feet high, with the sunshine making them sparkle till it hurts your eyes, and the colored lights turned on at night, and the splendid fireworks?"

Happy they are, starting off for this holiday. For where in all the world can you spend such a day as at Versailles? Where else can you see so celebrated a park and the great palace of Louis XIV, nearly half a mile long, with one series of splendid rooms opening out after another, with the famous hall of mirrors? The spacious courts, the gardens and lawns that were once upon a time a swamp, the fine avenues of stately trees, the gleaming, cross-shaped pond and the glorious fountains whose water came from a river turned out of its course, full ninety miles away, all this beauty and luxury that cost the ancestors of Lucien and Renée so much in heavy taxes—today all this belongs to them, to the people of France.

Yes, this is a holiday at Versailles. Over the three great entrance gates that now stand wide open the tricolor floats in the soft breeze. In the court of honor flags are flying, over the royal stables and the barracks, over the chapel and theater.

It must have been just such a beautiful, warm fourteenth of July in 1789. Then too flags were flying at Versailles, not these banners of red, white and blue, but the white flag of the Bourbon kings who had reigned in France for two hundred years. Soldiers of the royal Guards stood on duty at the palace gates. In the garden servants were making ready a fête for the beautiful young queen, Marie Antoinette—"Madame Deficit" many of the French called her, blaming her and her extravagant ways for all their misery and distress.

But twelve miles away in Paris there was no holiday feeling on that Tuesday. Over the city hung excitement and confusion—an excitement and confusion that had begun two days before and with each hour grew greater and wilder. Since Sunday men had not slept. All Paris was in the streets. In groups people marched and paraded and talked, talked, talked.

Now they stopped to listen to some street orator. Now they gathered in the gardens of the Palais Royal, the center for news and gossip. Standing on a table in front of the Café de Foy a young man began to harangue.

The failure of the harvest and the cost of a loaf of bread—the twenty-five thousand soldiers that the king has thrown around the city —liberty and the rights of man—monstrous taxes paid only by the poor—the privileges of the nobles who enjoy themselves while the people starve—all this he touched on while his listeners came and went.

"And now," cried the speaker, "here is this last news from Versailles. Louis XVI has dismissed the ministers who were friendly to the people. He's going to break up the National Assembly and rule himself, with the help of the nobles. If there's any resistance, he'll turn the guns of the Bastille upon the city!"

"The guns of the Bastille!" echoed the crowd.

"The hour has come. The hour has come for France! To arms!"

"To arms!" Men took up the cry till it echoed through the narrow streets. "To arms!" Again and again it sounded through the city.

"Where are arms to be had?" some one asked.

"At the Hôtel de Ville."

The officials there tried to shut out the mob. But in through the iron gates they rushed and took what muskets they could find—three hundred and sixty in all. In an arsenal they discovered a few more. Twenty-eight thousand they found at the Hôtel des Invalides. Even these were not enough, for every citizen was now a soldier.

Blacksmiths worked without ceasing. In a day and night they turned out fifty thousand pikes, for pikes were quicker to make than muskets.

Through all the hubbub of the restless crowds that scoured the streets, above the tramping of feet, above the beating of drums and the ringing of alarm bells in every steeple sounded that threatening cry: "To arms!

Give us arms!"   And then on Tuesday morning came a second cry: "To the Bastille!"

Already two groups of citizens had gone to that old fortress demanding arms from the governor DeLaunay. Through the porthole he refused.

Muskets and pikes and wooden clubs were distributed. The streets seethed and boiled with grim-faced men. No longer was heard the cry for arms. They said only, "To the Bastille!" Toward that old building in the east of Paris they made their way. It was not an orderly march of soldiers on parade, wheeling with brisk step, marking time. Men crowded along shouting and yelling. They were a living tide that during many years had ebbed, had slowly turned, and now with a new force swept toward the eight grim towers of the Bastille.

Here was an outlet for their fury. How they hated the sight of the fortress! How they hated its very name! For more than four hundred years it had stood there grim and forbidding, threatening the city. Long, long before a king of France had built it as part of the defenses of Paris. But for a century and more it had been prison rather than fortress—

a royal prison where the king or his minister or one of his favorites could send a man—innocent or guilty no one stopped to ask—send him there without trial and keep him there for years and years till he was quite forgotten. The Bastille was a symbol of the absolute power of the sovereign. To the people it stood for selfishness and injustice. It stood for oppression and wrongs unredressed for centuries.

And now on the fourteenth of July, 1789, the mob swelling ever wilder, shouting ever louder massed in front of the fortress. What could pikes and muskets do against walls nine feet thick? against cannon pointing down from the battlements?

What would DeLaunay do, that loyal old soldier whose orders were to hold his post? There were fifteen pieces of artillery on the tower platforms. His force numbered eighty-two Frenchmen and thirty-six redcoated Swiss. He had no store of food or ammunition. Should he surrender? The Bastille had resisted many an attack in the past. Should he fire on the mob? They were badly armed and leaderless.

It was one o'clock.

One hundred and eighteen against those

thousands boiling and whirling in a mad flood.
With smoldering eyes and clenched hands,
with a fury in their brains they besieged the
old fortress.   Every suggestion made by some
fellow in the crowd they caught up eagerly.

"Send for the firemen to wet the touchholes
of their cannon!"

This they tried.   But the pumps could not
reach so high.   They made only clouds of
spray.

"Burn some straw and smoke them out!"

Three cartloads of straw were brought from
somewhere, hauled into place, and the mass set
on fire.   White, white smoke went up almost
choking the besiegers.

"Drag up the cannon from the parade-
ground."

"What—the little silver-mounted cannon
sent to Louis XIV by the king of Siam?   Try
them.   But what can they do against those
massive bulwarks?"

All this time the firing of muskets never
stopped.   From behind battlements, from
portholes the besieged fired back.   The eighty-
three wounded were carried into nearby houses.

"Do not yield," they, cried, "till the strong-
hold falls!"

Climbing up on bayonets stuck into joints in the wall, two men struck with their axes at the heavy chains of the outer drawbridge. The iron links yielded, broke. The huge drawbridge thundered down.

Far below the prisoners in the Bastille heard a muffled din.

"What's happening out there?" they asked.

Vaguely the guards made answer.

DeLaunay was waiting for reinforcements. A troop of hussars crept cautiously along the river, coming up as close as the bridge.

"Alight and give up your arms!" called out one of the mob.

While the people cheered the soldiers of the king were disarmed and escorted back.

For four hours the firing kept up. Shots blazed and rattled, but fell harmless against the solid stone walls. DeLaunay would not surrender save at the king's order. He decided to fire the powder magazine and blow up the Bastille. But a soldier seized his arm and dashed to the ground the lighted torch.

By the inner drawbridge a porthole was opened. The Swiss guards hung out a white flag made of napkins. They beat a drum to ask a parley, but no one could hear.

"Safety for all if we surrender," they wrote on a paper and passed it out on the end of a bayonet.

"Yes—on the word of an officer," said the half-pay captain who led one portion of the mob.

The inner drawbridge was lowered. In rushed the besiegers. The Bastille was theirs!

It was twenty minutes of six.

Against the wall the hundred and eighteen piled their arms. Into the fortress plunged the mob. Through court and corridor they rushed, over bridges, down steep stairs, into dungeons and narrow cells.

"Take the governor and the other officers to the Hôtel de Ville," said the half-pay captain.

But the mob forgot the promise of safety, hustled them along and killed them in the street. Their heads were placed on pikes and carried along in triumph. Men and women looked on shouting, "Liberty forever!"

It was twenty minutes of six, the hour of the birth of liberty in France. The late afternoon sun shone on the garden fête at Versailles where officers and ladies of the court were dancing and feasting. It shone on the barracks full of soldiers drinking and singing.

Its slant rays lighted the babel and bedlam swarming about the old fortress. They shone on a procession that wound through the streets of Paris. Shoulder high the victorious mob carried the seven prisoners found in the Bastille. The light touched the scanty white hair of one of these poor men who for thirty years had lived in a cell and could not tell whence he came nor why he was a prisoner.

The sun shone too on rusty iron keys held up for the people to see. They were the symbol of the end of tyranny in France. It shone on a cage of iron, on heavy padlock chains torn from heavy doors, on monstrous blocks of stone and trap dungeons—things that for long years had not seen the light of day.

As twilight came the destruction of the Bastille went on rapidly. Great stones were wrenched from their foundations. Bit by bit the eight massive towers went down. The stern battlements that made a dark shadow over the city fell as pike and musket hammered at them.

"The building itself must be destroyed!" shouted the people. "Never again a king with such absolute power!   Never again such despotism in fair France!"

A small affair to destroy a fortress?

The fall of the Bastille was like a writing on the wall.   It marked the end of the old monarchy.   It marked the beginning of the new France.

"An evil omen," said king and queen and nobles.

"A good omen," said the people of France.

Through the great park at Versailles walk Renée and Lucien and Jacques.   From the terrace they watch the fountains play.   Awestruck they gaze about them in the hall of mirrors.   They look at the splendid paintings that tell, in room after room, the history of France. They stroll over to the little farm where Marie Antoinette played with her blue-ribboned sheep and made butter in the dairy-house while the king carried sacks of wheat to the mill. Here the court amused itself while the people were starving.

Under the trees the children listen to the story of that fourteenth of July, a tale that is old to every French boy and girl, but one they never tire of hearing.

"Why did they call it the Bastille?" asks
Renée. "What does it mean?"

"It means 'building'" replies her father.
"The people called it 'the building' as if there
were no other. But it was not with love they
christened the Bastille."

"When we go home," says Jacques, "will
you take us over to the Place de la Bastille?
I'd like to see it today."

So in the evening this French family walks
into the great square where once stood the
grim, old fortress.

"Is the great, high column in the center a
monument for the fourteenth of July?" the
children ask, craning their necks to see the figure of Liberty on the top.

"Yes, but years later than the fall of the Bastille. It's in honor of the heroes of the revolution of 1830. You see, there's nothing left
of the old building—no ruins, no great blocks
of stone, no iron cage. But look here!"

In the pavement near the Rue St. Antoine
the children find a line of white stones. Trac-
ing it back yard by yard they make out the site
of the Bastille. Here it ran close to the river.
There it curved out for one of the frowning
towers. They pictured the Place as it looked

on the fourteenth of July with loyal old De-
Launay refusing to surrender and the roaring
sea of men whirling and seething, shouting and
firing.

"For years and years," says their father,
"the people of France had been oppressed and
voiceless. In 1789 they found their voice.
And it was the voice of the people that took
the Bastille as once long before, in a land far
away the walls of Jericho fell at a sound."

THE FATHER OF FIVE
COUNTRIES

THE TWENTY-FOURTH OF JULY

"Only give us a leader! We too have patriots who dare to dream of liberty!"

"It's true, all you've said of this new interest
in liberty that's sweeping over the world. The
United States began it in '75. France beheaded her king. Greece is trying to free
herself from Turkey. It's reached even as far
as here in Venezuela. Give us a leader! And
Spain—"

"Yes," interrupted a third, "all of this
great continent, except Brazil, belongs to
Spain. And how does she treat us? She'll
learn nothing from England's bitter lesson in
North America. Only look at the amount of
taxes we pay—taxes we have no share in vot-
ing."

" 'Taxation without representation,' "
quoted one of his listeners, "that's tyranny!"

"And look at all the restrictions Spain

hedges about us—we can't grow almond trees or grapes, we can't make oil or wine, we can't weave cotton cloth, we can't trade with anybody, anywhere—save with certain Spanish cities—we can't hold an office. For what do we exist? Tell me that—for what do we exist?"

"To glorify the mother country," answered several voices.

"Yes, to glorify Spain," he repeated bitterly. "But give us a leader. Venezuela is seeking her George Washington. Who is her man-of-the-hour?"

The group of patriots was silent.

They had no leader.

"What would you think," one man spoke up timidly, "of interesting Bolivar?"

"What—young Simon Bolivar?"

"Who's he?"

"Where does he live?"

"I knew his father—years ago—a nobleman at our capital. The boy's an orphan and heir to vast estates near Caracas. But—lead a movement for our country's liberty? He's not interested in liberty. He used to like athletics and riding. Now he cares only for pleasure and travel. Abroad still, I believe."

"Yes, in Madrid, my agent there writes me. He's a great favorite at court. Plays tennis with the crown prince—and wins! There's something about it in the last letter. Wait, here it is."

He opened the pages and read aloud:

"Perhaps you'll be interested, Señor, in a bit of gossip about one of your fellow-citizens—the rich, young Bolivar who plays tennis here with the crown prince. Report has it that he said, 'Look out, your Highness, I give you fair warning. I've won from you at tennis. Some time I shall take your brightest jewel.' Is anything afoot in Venezuela?"

"Nothing's afoot till we find a leader."

Their talk drifted from Bolivar to the latest news from Madrid and Europe. No one in that group guessed that Venezuela's man-of-the-hour would prove to be the rich young noble, that his threat to the prince would come true and more, that he would take not one jewel only, but two, three, four, five. No one knew that a visit to the gay city of Paris had chanced to show him the last striking scenes of the Revolution.

Already he was dreaming of liberty for Venezuela, for the other countries of the great southern continent. Standing on one of the seven hills of Rome he had vowed to devote himself to that cause.

On his way home he traveled through the United States, anxious to see for himself how a government of the people was succeeding. This was the last step in fixing his purpose. He would free South America from the tyrant Spain and establish her independence,

By this decision Bolivar had everything to lose and nothing to gain. He might have been the richest, the most powerful of his class. He might have lived in luxury all his years. He might have had the favor of the court and of the king. All this he gave up to be true to the spirit of liberty in his soul.

In Venezuela he joined this group of patriots who were working toward independence. He was all for taking action at once. What matter how things went in Spain, in Europe? Some of his friends urged delay.

"You say great projects should be patiently weighed. Yes—but aren't three hundred years of waiting enough?"   And to those who argued that the mother country's plans must be considered he answered, "What shall we care if Spain chooses to keep us as her slave or sell us to Napoleon, since we have decided to be free? Let us fix without fear the foundations of our liberty."

In July of 1811 Venezuela proclaimed her independence from Spain. The following year war began in earnest. But the first attempts of the patriot group failed. Their republic was short lived. Bolivar escaped to the west and offered his services to the president of New Granada (the country that is now Colombia) where the revolutionists were for the time in control. With only two hundred men against an enemy ten times as strong he fought twelve battles in fifteen days and gained a large province for the patriot party.

He asked permission to invade his native state and argued that only through her independence could the freedom of South America be won. Indeed for their own safety the New Granadians must reconquer Venezuela or the Spanish would use it as a base of supplies against them. The permission was given and with four hundred followers Bolivar crossed the frontier.

A rash movement? He did not stop to count the odds against him. He called on all good citizens to aid. As he moved eastward the people rose in arms. Soon he had a thousand soldiers. After no less than fifty combats he entered Caracas in triumph.

His fellow-citizens gave him a great ovation. Girls strewed roses before him. The crowds hailed him as their deliverer, "el libertador." They voted that he should have all the powers of a dictator in civil and military affairs. But the Venezuelans were not ready for self-government after three centuries of Spanish rule. When Bolivar appointed his ministers he found that at every turn he must direct them all.

The Spaniards were not conquered. They sent a new army and defeated the republican forces. Bolivar fled to Jamaica. Not that he had given up hope of freeing his country. Not that he had abandoned his dream of liberty. He never despaired. He never lost heart. Later his enemies described him as a man more terrible in defeat than when he conquered. As he was leaving Venezuela he said, "There is no power in the world capable of arresting me in the work in which I am engaged. God reserves victory to constancy."

In Jamaica and on the island of Haiti he gathered the fugitive patriots together. They needed help of every kind—arms and ships and money. The negro president of Haiti welcomed Bolivar and gave him warm support in his struggle with Spain, but with one condition—that when success came he would free the slaves in Venezuela. He promised and loyally kept his word, more than forty years before Lincoln's proclamation gave freedom to the slaves in the northern hemisphere.

Another friend for the cause was found in Haiti, a Dutch ship-builder who fitted out seven schooners and gave also three thousand muskets. On the last day of 1816 Bolivar sailed back to Venezuela. He had three hundred men, the same number that marched with Leonidas, and his equalled that Spartan force in courage and patriotism. He issued a proclamation summoning representatives of the Venezuelan people to a general congress. Then he burned his seven ships. Now the adventure must end in success or death!

Spain had sent another army with orders to subdue the rebellious colonies at any cost. For a year Bolivar carried on confused operations against it. Then tired of aimless marchings and countermarchings he thought out a plan—a daring plan that needed desperate courage to carry through. In the history of the world there are only one or two exploits to compare with this.

There was little to be accomplished just then in Venezuela. In New Granada a republican army kept up the fight for liberty. Why not cross the mountains, unite all the patriot forces and push their enemy toward the northern hills and the sea? Success would come through surprise and the enthusiastic support of the people living in the territory to be invaded.

It was the wrong season of the year for such a crossing? Odds against him, odds of nature, odds in favor of the Spanish Bolivar never counted. He bent every energy to carry out his plan and promptly, before his foes should learn of it.

The first few days the march was across broad, open plains up to the base of the mountains. In the dry season a hard track led through waving grasses, past empty river beds, by knolls crowned with tall trees. Now the rainy season had set in. The flat country was flooded. Every little stream was a river. The knolls were islands. The hard track was liquid mud.

The little patriot army waded knee deep, waist deep. Scarcely stopping for an hour the rain beat down upon them. Each day they crossed a dozen streams, fording when they could, swimming, or ferrying themselves over in boats made of hides.

Once across the wide plains matters became not better, but worse. Great cascades tumbled down from the mountain heights. The road led along the edge of precipices. On one side it was marked by huge trees whose tops were lost in the mist. The rain kept on day after day. Up and up went the march.

Often the path was blocked by landslides. The men crossed raging torrents on tree trunks that shook with every step. Sometimes they made hanging bridges of hide-ropes lashed to either bank and went across in "cradles" each holding two soldiers. In his faded blue uniform with the red facings Bolivar passed and repassed these streams on horseback, always with a sick man behind his saddle.

Up and still up they went. The clouds were below them. There was nothing to see but huge rocks and masses of snow. The troops were used to the warm, moist air of the plains. Now they met cold fogs and a piercing wind that the stoutest clothing could not shut out.

A hundred soldiers of the enemy could have trapped them in those ravines. But Bolivar had not chosen the ordinary pass for crossing the Andes. Lest the Spanish might be expecting him he had turned to a disused track that led over a desolate height.

Complaints broke out. The men began to murmur. Would their hardihood fail now? A council of war was summoned. Frankly Bolivar talked with his officers.

"I will hide nothing from you. In all likelihood there are perils ahead of us worse than any we've encountered. Shall we go on? Or shall we abandon our attempt?"

"Forward!" came the answer.

Weary, exhausted they were still ready to follow him. At last the handful of wretched, famished men were across the pass. Before them lay broad valleys, green and fertile. They saw sunshine once more. The people of a village poured out to welcome them. They brought food and tobacco. The soldiers threw themselves down to rest in the sunshine and fell to polishing their rusty guns.

Bolivar had done the impossible!

Where the enemy least expected him he suddenly appeared. The Spanish general moved toward Bogota to avoid being cut off from the capital. The battle came at the bridge near Boyaca. Bolivar placed a large part of his force in ambush. When attacked the few visible troops gave way in a pretended panic. The enemy pursued. From both sides the concealed patriots rushed forth. The cavalry swept down from the rear. In two hours the day was won.

The Spanish general flung away his sword to avoid having to surrender it. He was taken prisoner on the battlefield with almost all of his officers and more than sixteen hundred men. The road to Bogota was open. Bolivar entered that capital amid the wildest rejoicings. New Granada was free!

Success in the west meant success in Venezuela. With united forces the patriot armies marched eastward. At Carabobo they defeated the Spanish by a clever flank movement over a wooded hill and through a ravine so choked with briars that the soldiers had to pass in single file. With the exception of one fortress the enemy had been driven from every post. Venezuela was free!

For the second time Simon Bolivar entered Caracas in triumph. Nor was this a temporary success like the other. A government was established uniting New Granada and Venezuela as the republic of Colombia. There was only one man to be president, Bolivar whom the people acclaimed as their liberator, the father of his country.

By 1823 he was free to help Ecuador and Peru, to complete the work of "saving a world from slavery." More than one great battle was fought before Spain would acknowledge herself defeated—the famous one of forty-five minutes at Junin where not a shot was fired, but the soldiers on both sides used only lance and saber; and the equally famous one at Ayacucho won by Sucre, Bolivar's second-in-command.

After two years of hard struggle Peru was free. She voted her deliverer a million dollars which he used to buy the freedom of one thousand slaves.

Next he must help the district called Upper Peru which later changed its name to Bolivia in his honor. He was declared "protector" of this new nation and the leaders asked him to draw up a constitution.   In reply Bolivar urged them to call a congress.

"A victorious soldier," said he, "does not acquire the right to govern."

For these new countries Bolivar dreamed great dreams, far-seeing visions of progress which even a century has not been long enough to see fulfilled.   He pointed out that their greatest need was popular education.   He proposed a fourth division of the government, a court to supervise the children's schooling and the maintenance of patriotism.   Its domain would be the public spirit, the hearts of citizens.

He dreamed too of a canal across the isthmus of Panama.   It would shorten the world's distances and bring to that spot the treasures of the seven seas.   It would be the site of a great city which should be the center of the universe, facing Asia on one side, Europe and Africa on the other.   It would be the seat of a supreme court guarding the interests of the two Americas.

In still another dream Colombia and Ecuador, Peru and Bolivia were to be united into a great federation of republics like the United

States.   It would reach from the Caribbean
Sea to the valley of the Amazon, from Atlantic
to Pacific.   But dissensions and jealousies
were rife among the people.   Instead of this
federation the union of Colombia and Venezuela crumbled during Bolivar's lifetime.

"I have ploughed on the sand," he said bitterly, heart-broken at the apparent failure of
his work.

Nine-tenths of his great fortune Bolivar
spent in the service of his country.   At one
time he controlled the revenues of three nations, but he never touched a penny of public
moneys.   He conquered wealthy provinces,
but refused to be more than their deliverer.
Half his salary as president of Colombia he
used for the widows and orphans of his
soldiers.

He was seized with a fatal fever.   Anxious
only for the state of the country he died saying, "Union! Union!"   The last of his inheritance had been used.   Friends had to meet the
expenses of his funeral.

More than once Caracas asked to erect a
monument in his honor.

"No," was his reply, "never raise monu-
ments to a man in his lifetime.   He may

change. He may betray. You'll never have to charge me with this. But wait, wait I say again. After my death you can judge without prejudice and accord what honors you think suitable."

With pomp and ceremony his remains were moved to his native city and a beautiful statue was erected. Today coins and squares, streets and towns and provinces in the five countries he helped to free, are called after him. His name and fame are everywhere throughout South America. And on this twenty-fourth of July Venezuela and Peru, Bolivia and Colombia and Ecuador, a territory two-thirds as large as Europe, keep his birthday.

THE VIGIL ON THE CARTEL SHIP

THE THIRTEENTH OF SEPTEMBER

"What's this you say, Mr. West? Dr. Beanes taken off in the middle of the night by the British? And they won't let you see him?"

"That's right. We thought, his friends and patients in Marlborough, that you were just the man to help us. You're a lawyer, Mr. Key, and the old doctor's friend. So I came out to Georgetown to tell you of his arrest and the rough treatment they gave him. I was certain you'd go."

"Go—go where? What can I do?"

"First, get a letter from the Secretary of State to Colonel Skinner, our agent for the parole of prisoners. Then go out to the British admiral under a flag of truce and intercede with him before the fleet sails. How could they break in at the doctor's house," West continued with growing indignation, "and drag him out of bed with hardly time to dress, and march him off to their camp astride a bareback mule? Why, Dr. Beanes has taken care of all our family for years. You remember what he did for the wounded after the battle of Long Island, and at the Brandywine in that first hospital Congress established? Surely you will go?"

"Yes," said Francis Scott Key, "I'll go. I'll do my best, though I warn you it's no easy task, nor pleasant either. But on what grounds did they take Dr. Beanes prisoner?"

"Well, Marlborough people say the old doctor and two friends were in the garden when a group of British soldiers, straggling marauders from the main army, broke in. I suppose they were elated over their victory of the day before. At any rate they were insolent and disorderly. On the doctor's complaint they were arrested and lodged in the Marlborough jail. One brawny fellow made his escape in the night and told Admiral Cockburn some exaggerated tale about how the doctor tried to poison them. So a squad of marines was sent to arrest him in revenge.

"But at their headquarters the British tell quite another story. They told us Dr. Beanes had been their host on their way down to

Washington and now had broken his parole. Just think—a man of honor like the old doctor breaking his word!"

With Francis Scott Key to decide on a difficult task was to set about it at once. He went to the State Department for the necessary letter. The next morning, the fourth of September, 1814 he left his home in Georgetown for Baltimore.

There he sought the help of Colonel John Skinner. No one knew exactly where the British fleet was—somewhere in Chesapeake Bay. They set sail in the *Minden,* the cartel ship, in search of Admiral Cockburn.

Traveling was far slower then than now. Under the best of conditions it took two days to sail down from Baltimore. It was probably the seventh of the month when the *Minden* neared the flagship of the enemy's fleet and the two Americans went aboard with a flag of truce.

Colonel Skinner was of course well known to the British officers. Politely they received their callers. But when Mr. Key told his errand the British admiral was in no mood to grant the request.

"No," he answered, "Dr. Beanes has in-

flicted atrocious injuries on His Majesty's
troops.   He deserves the most severe punishment.   He shall be hung to the yard arm of
the flagship!"

So coldly was the application received Key
feared his mission would fail.   But Mr. West
had chosen wisely.   Francis Scott Key was an
eloquent speaker.   He had a gracious manner, a pleasing personality.   He was, in short,
a southern gentleman, courteous and tactful.

Did he dwell on the respect which the whole
community felt for Dr. Beanes?   Did he argue
that a man of such character and standing
could not be guilty of these charges?   Or did
he rely on the letters Colonel Skinner brought
to some British officers from their comrades
wounded in the fighting a few days before—
letters which told the warm appreciation they
all felt for the careful treatment and the kind-
nesses the good doctor had showed them?

Whichever it was, Mr. Key was victorious.
The admiral promised to release Dr. Beanes.

"But," he added, "you can not go ashore
just now.   We're about to make an expedition.
We can't run the risk of your giving the enemy
any information of the preparations you've
seen or heard aboard our fleet.   Of course

we'll try to make you as comfortable as possible. I must apologize for not being able to
accommodate you here, but we're already
crowded. I'll transfer you to the ship my son
commands."

Colonel Skinner, Mr. Key and the old doctor, now a free man once more, sailed with the
British fleet and on the morning of the tenth
reached the mouth of the Patapsco River.
Then under a guard of marines they were
taken off to their own vessel, the *Minden*. By
the admiral's orders it was anchored where
they could watch the attack. They would be
eyewitnesses of the great British victory, of
the defeat of their countrymen.

Every movement of the enemy they observed and with anxious hearts debated the
outcome. They knew their militia had been
routed at Bladensburg. They knew about the
burning of Washington. They knew what defenses Baltimore had—earthworks hastily
thrown up east of the city, some vessels sunk
in the channel, and several small batteries
added to Fort McHenry, standing sentinel at
the mouth of the river. They knew what defenders the city had—raw militia to meet
trained and hardened veterans.

They knew too what a grudge the British had against Baltimore. "A nest of pirates," they called it and marked it out for special vengeance because it was the home of swift privateers that preyed on their commerce. Key knew that an English general had boasted, " I don't care if it rains militia! I'll take Baltimore and make it my winter headquarters."

Prisoners on an American vessel, the three watched for three days the landing of the British army of nine thousand. They saw the lines drawn up in hostile array at North Point, a dozen miles from Baltimore. From the road leading to the city they heard the booming of cannon, the roar of rapid-firing muskets. It was a calm September morning. The breeze brought the sound clearly. How was the battle going?

The Americans, they were to learn afterward, held the enemy in check. On the death of the British general the officer left in command hesitated to attack again. Why not wait till the fleet passing Fort McHenry could bombard the city and coöperate with the army?

But a hitch occurred in this plan.

Early on the morning of the thirteenth the

three watchers on the *Minden* saw sixteen vessels sail up and form in a great half-circle opposite Fort McHenry. Francis Scott Key and the doctor plied Colonel Skinner with questions, but he could tell them little. The fort was in command of Colonel George Armistead. He had perhaps twelve hundred men, counting three companies of volunteers from Baltimore.

"But why doesn't he fire back?" asked Key anxiously. "Hasn't he some finely placed batteries and heavy guns?"

"Yes. But the British are out of reach. See how far they stay, out of harm's way. They're a good two miles from the fort. But their bombs are reaching her. Here, take the glasses. Some pass over, but some are bursting right above the fort."

"Oh! Four or five all at once! It makes a double explosion. They're pumping their heavy bombs on our poor little fort, never stopping. But tell me, why do our men fire back now and again?"

"That's to let them know the garrison has not surrendered."

About three o'clock in the afternoon some of the British vessels moved in closer to the fort. Key saw them come within range of Armistead's guns. Bombs and shells hailed down upon them. His heart leaped as he watched the firing of his countrymen. How deliberately they were aiming! Every shot told. It must be getting hot for the enemy. In half an hour they slipped their cables and sailed back out of distance.

Later Key learned the cause of this. One of the American guns was struck and blown off its carriage. The flurry of caring for the wounded and remounting the gun made the British think there was great confusion in the fort. So they sailed in closer, but soon returned to a respectful distance.

After this little incident the fight went on as before. Keeping outside the range of the fort's guns the British threw bomb after bomb. The horrible clatter never ceased. Explosion followed explosion.

The hours went slowly by. The flag on the fort, Key saw with the glasses, drooped round its staff. But at twilight there came a cool, gentle breeze. The air stirred and caught its folds. In a last salute to the sun the stars and stripes unfurled over the ramparts of Fort McHenry.

Just then a shell pierced the flag. One of the stars was torn away. Key's eyes filled with tears as he saw it.

Night fell hiding the fifteen stripes of red and white, hiding the fifteen white stars on the field of blue. Bravely, defiantly the flag was flying in the face of English cannon. Would it be still flying when morning came?

The enemy's movements could no longer be seen. Worn out by the excitement of the day, the old doctor went below to rest. Colonel Skinner joined him. But Francis Scott Key had no thought of sleep. Anxious, wakeful he paced the deck of the cartel ship all night long. Wondering, praying he listened, listened to the firing which never stopped, to the occasional shot that answered from the little fort.

About one o'clock the noise increased. Key heard the British give three cheers. The American guns fired quickly over and over again. The enemy sent up rockets to guide the twelve hundred marines who were landing with scaling ladders to storm the fort in the rear. They made quick flashes of light here and there on the river, on the shore, and then went out leaving the darkness blacker than before.

Key watched this bombardment with bated breath, with throbbing heart.   There was shower after shower of shot from all the guns of the fort, from the batteries at the quarantine station, from the barges in the river.   The British fleet responded with entire broadsides. For two hours the sky was filled with flame and thunder.

The bursting of the bombs and the red glare of the rockets made the heavens aglow with a seething sea of fire.   The water of the harbor was lashed into angry waves.   The *Minden* tossed about as though in a tempest.

In the midst of the terrific explosions Key heard not cheering, but the cries of wounded and dying men.   Did they come from the fort? from the transports?   What did they mean?

Then came a sudden silence.

Not a shot was fired.   An awful, deathlike stillness reigned.   The suspense was unbearable.   Had Armistead and his men made a last gallant effort before they surrendered? Had the British abandoned the attack?

As long as the guns of the fort kept up their firing Key knew its defenders were undismayed. But this silence was ominous. Was it victory? He was afraid to hope. Was it defeat? The lonely man paced up and down.

The night sky gave no answer to his questions: Had Armistead surrendered? Were the British even then marching that short two miles into the city? When day came at last would they look out from the *Minden* on a scene of havoc and plunder and fire? Would the British flag or the stars and stripes be waving over Fort McHenry?

Anxiously Key looked at his watch. It must be nearly morning. Colonel Skinner joined him. In the sky came the first gray streaks of dawn. Over the fort hung a heavy fog of smoke and mist. It enveloped the harbor and lay close to the surface of the water.

At last in the east showed a bright line of gold and crimson. Another and another. In its full glory the sun rose. The mist over the river lifted. With the glasses turned on the little fort they could see a flag flying.

"Oh!" cried Key, "oh! It's the star-spangled banner!"

His words were exulting, like a prayer of praise and thanksgiving. His heart was bursting.

The stars and stripes caught the first gleam of the morning light. In the river red and white and blue were reflected as in a mirror.

The darkness and gloom of night were gone. The long vigil of the American on the cartel ship was ended. That flag waving in triumph after a steady bombardment of twenty-four hours told the whole story.

Baffled the enemy's fleet was drawing off. Soon after sunrise word came from the British to Colonel Skinner that the attack had failed. When their vessels had dropped down the river the Americans were at liberty to go ashore.

On the back of a letter Francis Scott Key wrote down his thoughts, the first lines of a poem. In the little boat that took the three up to Baltimore he finished the stanzas that filled his mind and heart. The next morning he showed them to a friend who liked them so much that he said, "We must have this printed without delay."

That night at a theater in Baltimore the

words were sung to a well known tune. Copies of the poem were handed out on the street. In an hour it was all over the city. Every one sang or whistled it. News of the British attack and the defense of Baltimore went speedily through the United States. With it went the song written by Francis Scott Key. In a fortnight distant New Orleans was singing "The Star-spangled Banner."

For more than a hundred years Americans have sung it and have loved it. Every word came warm from the heart of the man who witnessed that thrilling scene. Every word finds a response in the hearts of those who sing.

What a poem it is for spirit and for beauty! Written during all the excitement of battle, during the falling of shot and shell, of bombs and rockets, there's scarcely a word of fighting in its four stanzas. Written by a southerner, it has no hint of North or South, only of loyalty to the nation. Written by a man held by British orders there is no suggestion of triumph over an enemy. It is a prayer for the future of America, the land of the free.

This is the story of the glorious, faded, tattered flag with the fifteen stripes and fifteen stars, now in the National Museum in

Washington—the flag that floated over Fort McHenry in 1814. This is the story of the holiday celebrated each September in the state of Maryland.

ON THE JANICULUM HILL

This is a gala day in Italy. From Lombardy in the north to Sicily in the south the people are rejoicing. Red, white and green flags are flying everywhere—in Milan and Venice, in Naples and Palermo and Florence, in the little island of Caprera off the coast of Sardinia.

Nowhere is the holiday spirit more evident than in Rome. Soldiers and civilians throng that narrow main street called the Corso. The king is holding a grand review. The people cheer him as he rides along with his staff, cheer the Italian flag, cheer the gallant Bersaglieri, the king's own regiment in dark uniforms and broad-brimmed hats plumed with green cock feathers. Over and over again they call out, "Viva l'Italia! Viva l'Italia!"

As the king rides by the Janiculum Hill and the equestrian statue there, he bares his head in silent homage to that figure of a soldier

236

overlooking the city on the seven hills. The
crowds see his action and cry out again, "Viva
l'Italia e Victor Emmanuel!" And some of
them cry, "Viva l'Italia e Garibaldi!"

This gala day is not so old as many other
national holidays. Only to 1870 can it look
back, so new is Italy among the countries of
the world—the true Italy, once merely "a
geographical expression," a house divided
against itself, now united into one strong
government.

On the twentieth of September, 1870 there
was fighting in Rome. The French troops
who had for years been stationed there to
defend the pope were called home by the out-
break of the Prussian war. At last, at last
came the opportunity for which the patriots of
Italy impatiently waited. Victor Emmanuel
called upon Pius IX to surrender. Only to
force would the pope yield. The king directed
his army to march on the city.

Early in the morning the attack began.
The papal troops were very few. They were
powerless to resist fifty thousand trained soldiers. Near the Porta Pia a breach was made
in the walls. Crying "Viva Savoia!" the
king's men dashed through. By noon the

whole city was in their hands. At St. Peter's a white flag was hoisted.

After fifteen hundred years Rome had become the capital of a united Italy. Yes, for fifteen centuries her people had dreamed of this day—dreamed though foreign rulers tyrannized over them for a thousand years, dreamed though the country was broken up into a dozen little kingdoms, duchies, grand duchies and republics, an easy prey to stronger neighbors.

Not till the following June was the government moved from Florence to Rome. Not till then did Victor Emmanuel enter the city riding side by side with the man in the red shirt. Not till five months later did the first all-Italy parliament meet in the palace on the Capitol. The king opened its session saying, "The work to which we have devoted our lives is accomplished." He was interrupted by such a storm of applause that the cheering was heard in far distant streets.

But the people of Italy did not need to wait for these later events. When the Bersaglieri dashed through the walls of Rome on that twentieth of September, for them the dream had come true. And it is this date they have made their great holiday, celebrating the triumph of Italian unity.

To whom was this triumph due?

Some say to a short, thickset, little man with monstrous mustachios, Victor Emmanuel, the first king of modern Italy. He was the young duke of Savoy when his father abdicated and made him king of Sardinia. With good reason the soldiers loved him, for he was himself a soldier born and bred. During one battle when victory seemed to smile on the Austrians, sword in hand he rode toward a regiment, his eyes flashing, his mustachios bristling on end, and cried, "With me, Guards, to save the honor of Savoy!" The famous Zouaves were filled with admiration for his fiery valor when they saw him rally his men and lead a charge that gained the day.

Offered easier terms by Austria if he would recall the constitution granted by his father and fly the standard of Savoy instead of the Italian flag, he refused without a moment's hesitation. Boldly he affirmed that he would "preserve intact the constitution and uphold the tricolor, the symbol of Italian nationality which vanquished today will one day triumph." He must perforce accept the harsh terms of peace which Austria dictated. But he rode away from Novara waving aloft his sword and exclaiming in resolute terms, "Italia sara!" (Italy shall be!)

He won the confidence of his subjects by his strength of character and honesty of purpose. *Il re galantuomo,* the king who is a man of honor they called him, a title won by a lifetime's devotion to Italian liberty. Shrewd he was and bold, with dash and impetuous energy, always a man of his word. Yes, Italy owes much to Victor Emmanuel.

Some there are who think the credit goes to Mazzini, the poet and dreamer who at sixteen put on mourning for Italy and wore it for the rest of his life. Dreaming of a free and united country he organized "Young Italy," a society which in two years grew to sixty thousand and was perhaps the greatest one cause of final success. In the hearts of Italians it roused the spirit of nationality.

Mazzini was tireless in conspiracy. Exiled from his own land, driven from France and Switzerland he lived for years in England. Always he preached and taught freedom for Italy. Always he was plotting and counterplotting, urging and encouraging. It was he who planned the desperate raid (one of many such) which ended in Garibaldi's proscription. It was he who first told Europe, in a periodical he published in London and later in newspapers in Florence and Genoa and Turin, of the South American exploits of the man in the red shirt; and told them in such glowing colors that on his return to Italy Garibaldi found himself with a widespread reputation as a dashing, skilful leader. He had only to ask for soldiers and they rallied round him. Ah yes, to Mazzini, the soul of Italy, who breathed a new hope into his countrymen is owed more than can ever be repaid.

Some there are who say the triumph of September twentieth was due to Count Cavour, the constructive statesman of modern Italy. A newspaper editor, a practical farmer, a student and traveler, he became Victor Emmanuel's chief adviser. He was keen enough to see that Italy's independence could be won only through the conflict of her stronger neighbors. He was a master hand at diplomacy, at all the ins and outs of trading and negotiating.

But whatever steps Cavour took—courting the friendship of France, goading Austria into war—he kept his eyes always on the one goal,

Italy's freedom. Toward this single purpose he fused the hopes of Mazzini, the incredible leadership of Garibaldi, the king's enlightened patriotism. The whole responsibility of the government he carried on his shoulders. Men called him the brain of Italy. His health gave way so that he died at fifty. "If I had died instead," said Victor Emmanuel, "it would have been better for Italy." Yes, the new nation owes much to Cavour, the master builder.

But give as generously as you will their dues to brave and resolute king, to brilliant prime minister, to exile clad in black, his countrymen give a greater praise to Giuseppe Garibaldi, the sword of Italy. In all of modern history can you find a story as romantic, as full of chivalry and daring, of headlong courage and self-denial as the tale of the man in the red shirt?

Like all his family since the days of Columbus Garibaldi was bred a sailor. In eleven years he worked up from cabin-boy to master. He was only a lad when he sailed with his father to the mouth of the Tiber and the two went up to Rome. His imagination was fired as they walked through the streets breathing of twenty-five centuries of glory. He passed

ruins that told of imperial Rome, once mistress
of the world. He saw priests and monks and
cardinals and papal soldiers telling of
spiritual Rome and many years of church history. The memory of the city's former name
made him believe firmly in her future greatness.

Now he saw a third Rome sitting proudly on
those seven hills amid all the beauty and grand-
eur of the past. This was a Rome that few
men even dreamed of—the capital of a new
Italy, free from foreign rule, united. Boy as
he was he never forgot that suggestion, never
lost that vision.

He was as overjoyed as Columbus discover-
ing a new continent, when he was first put in
touch with "Young Italy." All his life he
took Mazzini as his guide and counselor, his
friend and teacher. He made one of a band
that planned a raid into Piedmont, was be-
trayed and outlawed, sentenced to be shot.
Disguised in an old suit of peasant clothes he
escaped into France and thence to South
America.

Now a cattleman, now a tutor in mathematics he fought with any group struggling
for freedom. A wild guerrilla warfare he

carried on, sometimes with a few score of followers, sometimes with a few thousand, but always against great odds. His name was a terror to the enemy on land and sea, His adventures totaled an incredible number, as exciting and thrilling as those of the Cid or Ulysses.

Shot down on the deck of his ship, for days at the point of death, in the intervals of delirium he set the course for his men who had beaten off their foes, but could not sail the vessel. He was taken prisoner and hung up by the wrists for two hours; later the man guilty of this torture fell into his power and was released without a word of reproach. He wandered for days in the forest. Shipwrecked he saved his life by his remarkable powers of swimming.

All reward for his services, money or grants of land, he refused. Yet he was so poor at this time that he possessed just one red shirt and the family went to bed at sunset to save candles. Always he dreamed of Italy free and united.

In 1848 Europe was quivering with excitement. France had declared herself a republic. From north to south Italy was straining like

a hound in leash. After more than a century
of the rule of the Bourbon kings Sicily re-
belled. The king of Sardinia granted his
people a constitution. Piedmont began war
against Austria.

News of all these movements reached a little
group of Italians, exiles and refugees in
Montevideo. Their dauntless leader Garibaldi had been dreaming and hoping for just
this opportunity. Fighting now for a province of Brazil, now for Uruguay he had formed
an Italian Legion of five hundred men, planning to use this force to help win the freedom
of their native land.

Eighty-five of this now famous Legion
sailed back to Italy, crossed the Apennines in
the teeth of snowstorms, and marched toward
Rome spreading the gospel of liberty through
the villages on their way. They were a gaunt
group dressed in the red shirts of South
American cattlemen, with pointed hats topped
with plumes, their legs bare, their faces tanned
to copper color. Riding down the narrow
Corso at their head was the outlaw Garibaldi
in his red shirt and long poncho of white lined
with red, with a bright handkerchief loosely
knotted round his throat. The crowds

shouted, "He has come! He has come!"

The pope had fled from Rome. Garibaldi was chosen a member of the assembly. Crippled with rheumatism he was carried into the hall by a staff officer, to be present when the Roman Republic was proclaimed. His was the first voice to cry "Viva la Republica!" For a brief time the dream of his boyhood, of Italy's resurrection was true.

The rulers of Austria and Spain and France and Naples joined forces to restore the pope. Garibaldi was placed in command of the city's volunteer defenders. Outnumbered more than three to one by an enemy supplied with cannon and munitions, his little force fought valiantly and well. How could so small a garrison maintain an eighteen-mile defense? By sheer weight of numbers the French broke through the city walls.

The assembly debated whether to surrender, die fighting from street to street, or escape to the mountains. Garibaldi was summoned from his post on the Janiculum Hill. Just as he was, his face streaked with sweat, his clothes stained with blood and dust, his sword so bent that he could not force it into the scabbard, he galloped across the Tiber and entered the hall. Surrender? What—surrender Rome? Never, never! Let government and army flee to the mountains. Wherever they went, there Rome would be! And so it proved though for years Rome lived in the hearts of a few exiles.

The assembly voted to surrender.

In the great square before St. Peter's Garibaldi hastily called his troops together and proposed that they march with him into the wilderness.

"A new war I offer you," he cried. "I can give you no pay, no rest, food where it can be found. I can give you hunger and thirst, forced marches, battle and death. If you love Italy in your hearts and not with your lips only, follow me."

A mad march it was, the wildest and most adventurous of many. Pursued by flying columns of French and Austrian and Neapolitan soldiers they fled through bypaths of the mountains, along the tracks of goatherds, using devices learned in South American wilds. Garibaldi gave up his plan to reach Venice and doubled back across Italy. Every day there were narrow escapes from discovery. At every step he carried his life in his hands. Finally he sailed in a fishing boat from a little

Tuscan village. Standing up in the stern he called back to his friends on shore, "Viva l'Italia!"

Asked to leave France, then Tunis, then Gibraltar, he crossed the Atlantic to New York and lived there for a year and more, earning his living making candles. Then off to sea again—to South America, to China, and so to England and back to Genoa. With a little money saved from his voyages he bought part of the island of Caprera, off the coast of Sardinia. He lived in a stone house built with his own hands. He tended his sheep and goats, tilled the fields, and taught his children to read. All the time he was listening, listening for the voice of Italy.

Her call came in 1859. With France as her ally Cavour began another war with Austria. Garibaldi was summoned to enlist and lead the volunteers. The Austrians were bewildered by the speed and the bold rashness of his movements. In mountains and plains, night and day he kept up his skirmishing. Pursued he slipped through the fingers of the enemy. Two great battles the allies won. Suddenly peace was made. There was nothing more that Garibaldi could do.

Lombardy, Tuscany and some of the small duchies joined with Piedmont, calling Victor Emmanuel the king of Italy. But much of the country was not free. Stretching from sea to sea, separating south from north were the papal states.

The next year an opening came. A slight change it seemed at first. The king of the two Sicilies died and his son, a weak and ignorant boy, succeeded. A revolt began in Palermo, was suppressed, broke out again. At his little island Garibaldi received a secret message to come at once to head the patriots of Sicily.

Early in May two ships sailed from Genoa in the night, carrying the man in the red shirt and the famous Thousand. They landed on the eleventh and took Palermo, fighting behind barricades from street to street, then Milazzo and Messina in one victory after another. At the cry "Italy and Victor Emmanuel!" men flocked to join this hero till his army grew from one thousand to twelve.

Thirty thousand troops opposing them? On they swept, crossed to the mainland and marched three hundred miles to Naples which the boy-king had left in hurried flight the day before. As snow melts before the summer sun the Bourbon armies melted before the very name of Garibaldi.

"The bullets we aim at him," complained the royal soldiers, "lodge in his red shirt and he shakes them out at bedtime. He's in league with the devil!"

"A saviour sent direct from heaven," the people called him.

A temporary government was organized and Garibaldi proclaimed dictator. These unusual powers he accepted only until the king of Italy could arrive. The Sicilian fleet he presented to Victor Emmanuel, at one stroke increasing the navy from five ships to ninety-five—a gift from the cabin-boy.

"Complete victory all along the line," Garibaldi telegraphed after his final battle with the Neapolitan army, a struggle that lasted for twelve hours. The king of Italy marched southward at this news, scattered the pope's forces and took possession of the papal states, except the city of Rome, then went on south to the frontier of Naples.

At the crossroads near the toll cottage a group of horsemen waited. A military band played the royal march announcing the king's arrival. Garibaldi rode forward and bowed low exclaiming, "I hail the first king of Italy!"

"How are you, dear Garibaldi?" said the king and shook his hand warmly.

Side by side, followed by their staffs rode the man in the red shirt and the king in resplendent uniform, on whom had been bestowed the crown of the two Sicilies with nine million new subjects. Trumpets blowing, banners waving they entered Naples together.

"Rome," argued Garibaldi, "belongs to Italy. Neither pope nor emperor has a right to keep me out of it."

King and prime minister however knew that they were not strong enough to organize the south of Italy and at the same time fight the French at Rome. Sick at heart that the conflict could not go on till the work was finished Garibaldi determined to go back to Caprera.

They offered him the rank of marshal, the cross of a famous order, a pension of half a million francs, the title of prince, a dowry for his daughter, honors for his sons, a castle, an estate, a steamer for himself. As he had refused rewards and honors in South America he refused them now. What cared he for wealth, for titles? This man who might have been a king lived one degree above the peasants. He asked only to win Rome for Italy.

The Thousand crowded around him to say goodbye. Many of them were sobbing. Garibaldi's voice shook as he said, "Thanks! You have done much with scant means in scant time. But more is yet to do. We shall meet on the road to Rome. Farewell."

Poorer than when he left his island, for the equipment of the Thousand had been largely at his own expense, the man in the red shirt returned home. His secretary anxiously told him of the state of his pocket-book.

"Don't be worried. We have plenty of wood and corn which we will sell."

As months went by and nothing was done Garibaldi grew impatient. Crying "Rome or death!" he gathered a band of hot-tempered radicals in Sicily, crossed to the mainland and started north. Italy was at peace with France. She could not countenance such an attack. The King's troops met Garibaldi near Reggio and bade him withdraw. Shots were fired. The man in the red shirt was wounded and taken prisoner.

Another war with Austria gave Venice back to Italy. Still impatient Garibaldi tried once more, but his rash enterprise was defeated by the French. Not until September of 1870 did the king's army enter the eternal city. Garibaldi's dream of Rome as capital of all Italy, the dream of the boy, the dream of the exile riding across South American plains, the dream of the soldier defending his post on the Janiculum Hill had come true.

Speaking one day of the deliverance of Italy Garibaldi remarked, "Some men attribute success to Victor Emmanuel and some to Cavour and some to the great Mazzini. There are even those who give me the credit. But it was not the work of this man or of that. We all did our best."

It has become the custom, a custom that will some day be a beautiful tradition, that when the king of Italy passes the statue on the Janiculum Hill he takes off his hat in silent tribute to the man in the red shirt. As Rome was to Garibaldi the symbol of united Italy, to Italians he himself is now this symbol. For he loved his country not with his lips only, but in his heart.

THE STRANGER IN THE
THREADBARE CLOAK

THE TWELFTH OF OCTOBER

Very early one Friday morning in the autumn three ships sailed close to a little island in the West Indies. A boat was launched. A group of men rowed toward the shore.

With banners and flags they landed, flags with a green cross on one side and on the other the letters F and Y embroidered in gold. The leader, a tall man in a scarlet cloak with flowing white hair and keen, gray eyes, drew his sword and held it high.

"I take," he said solemnly, "I take possession of this land for Castile. It shall be called San Salvador."

Kneeling he kissed the earth and with tears gave thanks to God. The simple ceremony was over.

Now the arrival of these men with waving banners had not been unnoticed. Out from the distant trees the natives of the island came running to see the strangers. They were dark-skinned and half naked, with their bodies painted or greased. They were amazed at these intruders whose faces were so white, who wore such curious clothes covering all their bodies except hands and faces.

As the newcomers walked a short distance along the shore the natives turned and ran, then came slowly back. They were reassured by nods and smiles. Coming close they touched the white skin as if to make certain that the strangers were real and not a vision.

The leader offered presents—glass beads, hawks' bells, red caps. The dark-skinned islanders in return gave him tame parrots, some cotton yarn, a few small, gold ornaments. At sight of these the eyes of the captain gleamed. Eagerly he motioned, asking by a gesture where they found the gold.

In the south, they pointed.

"Ah," said the leader with a sigh, "this is only an island north of Japan. It has beautiful trees and shrubs. And gold's near by!"

For eighteen years this white-haired man, the son of an Italian weaver, had been dreaming and hoping and working to accomplish his purpose. And now he was here!

Yet things were not just as he had expected. Where were the riches of Cathay and India? where the great cities with palaces roofed with gold and bridges of costly stone, and crowded wharves with the vessels of all the world loading rich spices and gold and pearls? where the kings of strange eastern lands? These frightened, child-like red men—who were they? Some tribe of Indians they must be.

The new world to which these three ships had sailed was not in 1492 the world of the twentieth century. Its only people were savages who lived by hunting and fishing, who carried on a cruel warfare with neighboring tribes, who journeyed from island to island in rude canoes hollowed out of logs.

And the old world from which the three ships had sailed was not the Europe of today. Its people were living at the end of the Middle Ages, just rousing to discovery of new lands. There was a fever of excitement in the air. This was especially true in the town where lived the clothweaver and his sons. Back and forth over the Mediterranean sailed the ships of the merchants of Genoa, bringing from the eastern end of that inland sea rich cargoes that had been carried overland by caravan from the far east.

Beautiful silks and embroidered robes, fine weapons, spices and pepper greatly prized for seasoning the plain, coarse food of that day, these the boy Columbus saw unloaded. What stories he heard from the sailors—of pirates who attacked trading ships and stole their goods, of the Turks who had conquered the lands at the end of the Mediterranean and forbade all trade.

The sea was the only highroad to fame and fortune. With business ruined by the Turks many Genoese sailors and mapmakers went to Portugal. Her mariners were at that time the best in Europe. They had discovered more new lands—islands to the west, sections of the African coast that took them farther and farther south, farther as they hoped on the water route to India. With the other Italians went two sons of this poor weaver.

As he pored over his maps and read books about geography, books that you can see now in Spanish libraries with his notes in the margins, Christopher Columbus was thinking out his great scheme. He believed that the earth was round, not flat. Estimating its size as much less than it really is, he argued that the shortest way to the east was to sail west. He tried to prove this on a map, but said, "It shows more plainly on a sphere."

Such a voyage was practical, he reasoned, for there were islands all the way along—stepping stones to India. Off the coast of Asia Marco Polo said there were seven thousand islands. Why not sail west and reach the east? And who better than Columbus himself could captain such an expedition? Not many men of that day were so well educated. He read and wrote Latin and Italian, Spanish and Portuguese. Maps he made, beautiful and accurate. He knew mathematics and astronomy and the art of navigation. He had the imagination to plan this voyage and the boldness to carry it through. He had one other quality—persistence, a bull-dog hold-on-to-one-idea that would not let him relinquish it though years went by before he could get the help he needed.

For such a voyage he must have stout ships and brave crews. Ships cost money. Sailors must be paid wages. Where secure them?

First Columbus asked his home town. Genoa was busy with a war and would do nothing.

Then he went to the king of Portugal. He explained his scheme and pointed out that a sea route to India would secure for some country the rich trade with the far east. He asked for ships and sailors, and for himself a large share of whatever wealth might be obtained from his discovery and the governorship of the lands found. The Portuguese refused.

Might it be worth while to test out this Italian's scheme? The king sent some ships to the Cape Verde islands and gave his captains secret orders to sail on westward into the Atlantic to search for islands, stepping stones to India. Frightened at the great waste of ocean around them the Portuguese sailors soon turned back and ridiculed the plan. Sick at heart at such deceit Columbus went to Spain.

He supported himself by selling maps and books. Ever before him he kept his purpose of a voyage westward. Men laughed at him as a dreamer. Children poked fun at him. He went about so ill-clad that he was called

"the stranger in the threadbare cloak." But
the scheme had gripped him and would not
let him go. It was the passion of his life—
to sail west and reach the east, to get great
riches from its trade, to govern those strange
lands. He could not give up.

For eight years Coumbus talked over his
great scheme—talked to anybody who would
give him a hearing, to wise men from the court
and university, to the queen's advisers. They
listened and asked many questions. Some
laughed at his notions and declared him a wild
dreamer. Some touched their foreheads to
show that he was crazy. Some said, "If the
earth is a sphere there's no answer to your
argument about east and west. Spain would
be the richest country in the world if she'll
only fit out the ships, supply the sailors, and
send you on this great voyage of discovery."
But nothing was done.

Planning then to seek help in France
Columbus went down to the south of Spain to
get his little boy who since the mother's death
had lived there with an aunt. Near the town
of Palos the two stopped at the convent of
LaRabida. The father asked for a crust of
bread and a cup of water for the child. The

prior noticed the white-haired stranger at the gate, shabby but with a noble air, speaking Spanish with a foreign accent. He invited Columbus into the convent and talked with him.

Here was an interested listener. He asked many questions about the plans for this voyage and learned that though discouraged the stranger still believed in it. The good prior proposed writing to the queen whose confessor he had been, urging her to undertake the expenses of the expedition. Would Columbus and the boy wait there till the letter could be sent and an answer received? Yes, they would wait.

In a fortnight the messenger returned bringing orders for the prior to come to the queen at once. Shortly he was back, with money to provide a court suit for Columbus and a mule for the journey. His friendship was worth more than that of all the wise men of Spain.

The queen Isabella resolved to send Columbus on this voyage. But when they came to talk over the details she was amazed, as had been the Portuguese, to learn his demands— the governorship of all lands he might discover

and a share of their riches and trade. Eight
years of poverty and waiting had not been long
enough to change his mind.

"No," said the queen, "you ask too much.
We refuse all help."

Sadly, wearily Columbus turned away. He
would offer to France the discovery of a new
route to India. Surrender his plan? Give
up? Never!

Now the queen's treasurer and his friends
were distressed that France should have the
glory and riches resulting from this voyage,
all because Spain would not risk what seemed
a small amount of money, about sixty thousand
dollars. They went to Isabella, for they'd noticed that she was much more interested in the
plan than King Ferdinand was. Again they
told of the wonderful riches of the east, of the
honor and wealth that would come to Spain,
and urged her to equip the expedition.

"I will do it," she said decisively. "I will
get the money from my own kingdom of Castile."

By furious riding the royal messenger over-
took Columbus jogging along on his mule six
miles from Granada.

"Return at once. The queen commands it.

She and the king agree to all your demands."

First to get the ships. The little town of Palos had offended the rulers of Spain. As a punishment it was ordered to furnish Columbus two ships and their crews. A third vessel he got in Palos.

Next the sailors. He offered the wages paid on warships, a sum higher than other captains gave. He promised too four months' pay in advance. But nobody wanted to go with him. Men were afraid of dangers lurking in unknown seas. They'd never see their homes again. Prisoners were released from jail if they would sail with Columbus. Debts were forgiven if the debtors would join his expedition. Finally crews of ninety were secured.

Half an hour before sunrise on the morning of the third of August, 1492, the three ships lifted their anchors, spread their sails and headed out to sea from the harbor of Palos. They were within sight of the friendly convent of LaRabida. The shore was lined with men and women weeping and wringing their hands, bemoaning the fate of the doomed sailors.

Such little vessels they were. The flagship, the *Santa Maria,* was just over sixty feet in length and twenty wide; a dull, slow sailer,

Columbus complained, not suited to his purpose.   The *Nina* and *Pinta* were even smaller and open in the middle.   With a good wind they might make twelve miles an hour.

West to the Canary islands went the three ships, stopped to mend a leak, repair a rudder, and change sails.   Then with fresh water and supplies of food and wood, on the sixth of September they started westward again over wholly unknown waters.   The hearts of those rugged men failed them as land disappeared from view and they wept like children.

No one had ever gone so far west before. Therefore the ocean must be filled with countless dangers.   They were superstitious and feared the great monsters that lived in the Sea of Darkness, as they called the Atlantic.   Day after day the wind blew from the east.   This hastened their voyage, but made them fret over the difficulty of sailing home again.

The behavior of the compass alarmed them. As they went on it pointed not west of north, but exactly north and finally a bit to the east of north.   When the pilots found their faithful guide acting so queerly they cried out, "It's bewitched!   It plays these foul tricks to punish us for our boldness.   All the laws of nature are changed in this topsy-turvy world!"

For some days the ships sailed through great masses of seaweed—weeds as thick as a man's thumb and very long. Would they get entangled so they could not get out? Were these river weeds from some land not far away? Why not stop and search for it?

"No," said Columbus firmly. "We are sailing to the coast of Asia. Stop perhaps on the return. But now west, west, west! Sail on, sail on! Nothing shall delay us."

Late one afternoon the lookouts saw what appeared to be a coastline. It was really heavy banks of clouds. In the morning the mirage was gone.

"The place is enchanted!" they cried.

Day after day the sun rose out of the water. Night after night it set again in the ocean. Westward, always to the west Columbus set the course. His men despaired, hoped, despaired the more. They urged him to return. Among themselves they suggested pushing him overboard. But how could they sail back to Spain without him?

"Impossible to start back now," he said. "What would the king and queen say if we failed to go just a little farther? Land must be near. It must be. If we keep on we'll reach the coast of Asia and that will make us all rich."

Hope sprang up again when on the third of October they saw branches floating by, branches that bore red berries. Four days later the *Nina* which happened to be in the lead, fired a gun and ran up a flag—the signal agreed on when land was sighted. Again a mistake. Flocks of birds were seen. There were stories of Portuguese explorers who followed birds and found land. Some of them lighted on the masts and sang. Impossible for such tiny creatures to venture far, the men argued, and not be too exhausted to sing.

There was constant watching in the west. Every sailor was anxious to win the prize offered to the first person who sighted land. On the night of the eleventh, straining his eyes in the darkness Columbus saw a light moving up and down, disappear, come into view again. Was some one running along the shore with a torch?

"Land ho!" the lookout's voice rang out at two in the morning. A gun was fired. There it lay before them, vague and shadowy, but land, undoubtedly land! To avoid running ashore in the night time the sails were furled, the prows turned to the east.

Did any man on board sleep between two o'clock and dawn? What would day show them—the true coast of Asia with great cities and untold riches? gold enough to make their fortunes?

The voyage was over. The dream of Columbus was an accomplished fact. They had found the same kind of sea they were used to near Europe. The Atlantic was as calm as the Guadalquiver at Seville. Not one strange event had occurred. Portuguese sailors had more than once made longer voyages than thirty-six days. But this one stood out from all the others of that age: Columbus had sailed straight west two thousand miles farther than any ship had ever gone before. To the world he gave new continents.

Morning came. The Spaniards saw before them a beautiful, low island. With banners flying they claimed it in the name of Castile.

For three months they cruised about sailing along the coast of Cuba and Haiti. This the natives called Cibano.

"Cipango!" exclaimed Columbus, "Cipango! Marco Polo's name for Japan!"

They traded with the natives.   Always they looked, looked for gold.   On Christmas day the *Santa Maria* ran aground on a sandbank and was wrecked.   From her timbers a little fort was built on the north coast of Haiti. Forty men were left to hunt for gold and spices.

"I shall expect you to have two thousand pounds of gold by the time I return," Columbus told them.

A stormy voyage they had back to Spain. The two little ships were separated and met again in the harbor of Palos.   So fearful was Columbus that none of them would be saved. in all the fury of the tempest he wrote out the story of his voyage—the time it occupied, the lands and people he had seen, his danger at that moment.   He addressed it to the king and queen of Spain.   He wrapped it in a waxed cloth and placed it in a small barrel which he threw overboard.

A duplicate copy he put in another barrel on the deck of his ship so that it would float off if she sank.   If they were all lost at sea perhaps the record would be found.   He did not want future voyagers to imagine they had come to some mysterious end and be forever afraid to follow in their track.

On the fifteenth of March Columbus sailed into Palos. The bells were set ringing. Every one rejoiced at the return of the men whose start they had watched with cries and lamentations. What a story the voyagers had to tell! How the people crowded down to the wharf to gaze wondering at the Indians and the curious products of far-away lands!

From the court came orders for Columbus to come at once to Barcelona and report on his expedition. Slowly he traveled because of the crowds of people who thronged about him. At the head of the procession were six red men in feathers and war paint, wearing ornaments of gold. Then came forty porters each carrying a parrot in a cage, and other strange birds with brilliant plumage. There were men with branches of trees which were supposed to furnish spices.

At the end came Christopher Columbus on horseback and many Spanish nobles with him, making a gorgeous cavalcade. Thus the stranger in the threadbare cloak returned to court. He was no longer a poor mapmaker urging an impossible scheme for which he demanded ships and men.   He was a great discoverer who had brought glory and honor to Spain, and riches, riches!

Under their gilded canopy king and queen and prince stood up to receive Columbus, a mark of special respect shown only to royalty. They motioned for him to be seated while he told the story.   The Indians, the trinkets of gold, the pearl oysters, the parrots and branches were all brought into the court.   To each in turn Columbus pointed as he described the pleasing climate of this western land, the air filled with fragrance, the beautiful birds and flowers, the great wealth he thought the natives possessed, only a taste of the riches to come.   King and queen and all the court fell on their knees while the choir in the royal chapel chanted the *Te Deum*.

For six weeks Columbus stayed in Barcelona.   He was treated like one of the royal family.   He rode with the king and prince. People saluted him on the street.   Great nobles of Spain paid him court.   Ferdinand gave him a coat of arms which made him too a noble.   He was the greatest man in Spain.

Who could know at that time that Cuba was

not the mainland, but an island? that gold and silver would be found later in Mexico and Peru? that the crops of tobacco and cotton and potatoes which Columbus reckoned of little value, would give the world greater riches than all the gold Spain would ever get from mines in the new world? Who could foresee all the results of this voyage?

"Easy enough to find a water route to India," said a guest at the cardinal's banquet given in honor of Columbus. "All one has to do is to sail far enough west. If you hadn't discovered the Indies wouldn't some one else?"

The Italian's answer was a question. "Can you make an egg stand on end?"

Man after man tried. All failed.

"Easy enough." Columbus took up the egg, crushed one end a little, and made it stand alone. "Perfectly easy when some one else has once done it, señor!"

Preparations for the second voyage were begun without delay. Not three, but seventeen ships were provided. But the story of this and of the third voyage, when the mainland of South America was discovered, and of the fourth are not such pleasant reading. Columbus found the Haiti fort in ruins; all his men had been killed in return for the cruel treatment they gave the Indians.

Discontent broke out and grave sickness. Plots were hatched against the governor. The unceasing search for gold brought small results. The enemies of Columbus reported to the court that the colony was mismanaged. An officer was sent to decide between him and the leader of the rebellion. With no chance to tell his side of the story the great discoverer was placed in chains and sent back to Spain.

By Ferdinand's orders the chains were removed at once. Columbus was received again at court. But his governorship of the Indies was ended. The king made promises and did nothing.

The health of Columbus was undermined by hardships. He felt that he was neglected and unjustly deprived of his rights. In the house still shown to visitors, number seven in the Street of Columbus in Valladolid, the great voyager died. Save by a few close friends his illness and death were unnoted. The new world was not even named for him.

Four centuries after 1492 the country which he discovered held in his memory a world exposition, the greatest ever known. Year after

year on this twelfth of October Spain ob-
serves a holiday. Italy keeps it and flags are
hung out in the seaport of Genoa. The
United States celebrates it, honoring a man
not born here, a man who never even heard
of such a country. Ten nations in South
America observe it, though their very names
he did not know.

Three continents keep this holiday, paying
tribute to the son of an Italian weaver, a man
who had faith and courage and perseverance.

THE MAN WITH THE DARK LANTERN

THE FIFTH OF NOVEMBER

Above the noise of the town sounded the boys' voices.

> Oh, don't you remember
> The fifth of November,
> The gunpowder treason and plot?

The group suddenly turned the corner of a narrow, crooked street near the old walls of York. They walked briskly along half singing, half chanting their old rhyme:

> There is no reason
> Why the gunpowder treason
> Should ever be forgot.

"Remember Guy!" they cried. "Pray, sir, remember Guy!" Two or three of them held up their caps for pennies. "Please to remember the bonfire!"

274

"Guy? Bonfire?" questioned the American as he hunted in his purse for sixpences. "Guy? who in the world is Guy? And why a bonfire on so mild a November day?"

"You're from the States, sir, I'll wager," said one of the lads. "Don't you know about Guy—Guy Fawkes? Do come down to High Petergate tonight and see us burn him. Near the minster, you know. We'll tell you the story then. And thanks for the money. It's just what we needed for Guy's lantern. Ho there, wait for me!" Off he ran to join the others down the lane.

> Don't you remember
> The fifth of November?

Their voices sounded more faintly. Then the chant stopped. They appealed to the passersby to remember Guy. Pennies received, they took up the rhyme again.

> This is the day that God did prevent
> To blow up his king and parliament.

By eight o'clock that evening the American was on hand in the crowded square near the old minster. What a merry mood every one was in! The people waiting set off fire-

works. Some of them sang, the same old
rhymes the boys had sung earlier in the day.

Presently the procession appeared. Boys,
boys, more boys! They were shouting and
singing, pointing in scorn to the great Guy
who was carried in their midst. By chance
the line halted in front of the very spot where
the American was standing so that he had a
good look at Guy and the children marching
with him on a twentieth century fifth of November.

What an absurd sight Guy Fawkes was!
In America he'd be called a scarecrow surely.
He was lifesize, made of straw and dressed in
nondescript, old clothes. His face was a
comic mask with a long, red nose. On his
head was a paper cap wound with bright ribbons. In one hand he had a bunch of matches,
in the other a dark lantern. Thus he was
paraded through the streets of York, sitting
in state in a great chair, while the crowd
shouted and jeered and the boys, their arms
full of firewood, sang again:

> The fifth of November,
> Since I can remember,
> The gunpowder treason and plot.

The enormous pile of wood in the square was lighted. The flames shot up crackling and roaring. With shouts of glee the boys carrying Guy's chair pushed their way up and dumped him into the bonfire. And while the effigy burned they sang and danced around it.

> There is no reason
> Why the gunpowder treason
> Should ever be forgot.

Nor will it as long as the fifth of November is celebrated by English schoolboys. For more than three hundred years this has been a holiday in England, set aside by Parliament in 1606 as "a holiday forever in thankfulness to God for our deliverance." Every British child knows the exciting story of Guy Fawkes and the gunpowder plot. Here it is as a group of boys in York, Guy's birthplace, told it to a visitor from the States.

When James I came to the throne Parliament House stood by the Thames River at Westminster—of course not the stately buildings that are there today. At the south-west corner was a little two-story house where lived old Master Whynyard, the keeper of the king's wardrobe.   Most of the time he was away at court, so he agreed to rent his house to Thomas Percy.

But Percy didn't think up this plan.   It was Catesby, a Roman Catholic who was bitterly disappointed when James I enforced the strictest laws against people of that religion— laws that put priests to death for celebrating mass and made men pay heavy fines for not going to the Church of England services.

So he thought out a plan—the most desperate, terrible plan in all history!   He'd take vengeance on king and Parliament who were responsible, he thought, for these cruel laws. At one blow he'd destroy them all—King James and the Prince of Wales, the lords and bishops, the members of the Commons, the king's ministers.   When they were all present at the opening of Parliament he'd blow them up with gunpowder!

What would happen then?

With the government all in confusion the Catholics would rise and proclaim a new king in England—Prince Charles or else his sister Elizabeth.   And this child would rule with Catholic advisors.   They would have all their

old rights again. Their religion would be restored.

Some such plan Catesby worked out. To
four good friends he told it. They kept the
secret well. They met at night in Catesby's
house in Lambeth—just across the Thames
from Westminster. They talked over their
scheme in mysterious whispers. They were
bound by an oath not to speak of it.

It was the spring of 1604 when Percy hired
the house. Parliament was to meet the following February. It was none too soon to be
making their plans. Little by little they must
purchase what they needed. But they must
not meet too often. They separated and spent
the summer at different places in the country.

The early winter found them back again in
London. In December they began living in
the Westminster house. The first part of that
month they set to work. What a task they
had before them—to tunnel through from
Whynyard's cellar to the space under Parliament House!

The wall proved to be twelve feet thick.
Digging and toiling in the dark cellar was a
dismal job. Only two could work at a time

in the narrow space. Moreover they were gentlemen by birth and education. They were wholly unaccustomed to manual labor. At the end of a fortnight they had accomplished almost nothing at all!

Catesby had thought of everything. He had laid in a store of food so that they would not arouse suspicion by going out to buy provisions. He had provided lanterns and candles and tools—spades, pickaxes, augers, mattocks. In his house at Lambeth were thirty-six barrels of gunpowder, ready to be brought over the river and stored in the cellar till the fatal day should come.

A few more men Catesby had let into the plot till there were thirteen in all. One was Guido Fawkes, a Yorkshireman he'd met in Holland, a soldier of fortune in the Spanish army. "A man who knows his work," Catesby described him to the others. "I've chosen him to prepare the mine."

Day and night the conspirators labored. But a wall of solid masonry was not easy to mine. The stones were as hard and unyielding as iron. In many places the mortar was harder than the stones. Underground, with only dim lanterns to guide them they dug on;

with hushed speech, with such a fearful secret on their minds!

One day they were startled at hearing voices on the other side of the wall. Catesby fancied he could hear people moving about.

"Who can it be? I thought only great, empty vaults were there. Here, Guido! Run up to the street and keep your eyes and ears open. Bring us word what you find."

The tall, dark Fawkes threw down his pick-axe and went up the cellar stairs. With a question to this man and that he soon learned about the building next door. Under Parliament House were coal cellars. They were rented by a Mr. Skinner in King street. His men were taking away some coal that had been stored there. That explained the rumbling noise just over their heads, and the voices.

The plotters whispered, "If we could only get possession of Skinner's coal cellars! Then we needn't tunnel through this endless wall. We could easily be ready by February."

At last Percy hit upon a plan. Going to Dame Whynyard he told her his wife was coming up from the country. There wasn't half room enough for all her packages and boxes.

Couldn't the good lady help him out? If she could hire space from that coal merchant he'd give her something handsome for her trouble. Dame Whynyard agreed to try. For seven pounds, a year's rent, the conspirators secured the cellar.

A few at a time, at dead of night the barrels of gunpowder were brought across the river and stored in Skinner's space. Large stones and bars of iron were thrown in to add to the effects of the explosion. Then the whole mass was carefully covered up with coal and fagots of wood.

Prowling about Westminster Guy Fawkes picked up the news that King James had postponed the meeting of Parliament till the autumn. The day was set for the third of October. Once more the plotters separated and went off to the country for the summer months.

Again the opening of Parliament was put off till the fifth of November. The conspirators' plans were all completed. Catesby had bought a ship which was anchored in the Thames ready to sail, so after the firing of the mine Guy Fawkes could escape to Flanders. He had supplies of arms and relays of horses so that his friends could ride through the country to rouse the Catholics.

When the group met there was only one matter to be discussed. What should they do about their Catholic friends who were members of Parliament? Must they be blown up with the rest? Why not save their lives? Why not tell them to stay at home on the fifth of November?

"No, no," protested Robert Catesby, "that's risking too much. For the success of the plot, for the good of the Church they must be sacrificed."

"Yes. Our private feelings must be sacrificed for the general good."

"But think! What a terrible waste of life!" said Tresham.

"What matter if a few perish, if only our religion is restored? Rather than that our project should not succeed," cried Catesby, "if they were as dear to me as my own son I'd still say, they must be blown up!"

This decided word ended the discussion. But Francis Tresham could not forget that his sister's husband was a member of the House of Lords. How could he keep silence and let his brother-in-law walk into such a trap? Many an Englishwoman would grieve on the fifth of November. But of his sister's sorrow Tresham could not think calmly. Somehow Lord Mounteagle must be warned.

Now the books of history do not agree about Tresham. Some say he kept the secret to the end and did nothing whatever to betray it. Some say he loved Mounteagle and was determined to save his life. And still others declare that he was sick of the gunpowder plot and of his guilty part in it; that he was ready to do anything in his power to make it fail; and that the best way to save all those lives and his fellow-conspirators as well was to notify some member of Parliament of the danger.

On the twenty-sixth of October Lord Mounteagle was dining at his country home at Hoxton. A servant came in with a letter.

"What is this?"

"A stranger left it," was all the servant could tell.

Lord Mounteagle broke the seal and unfolded the single sheet of paper. Strange— there was no signature. There were no capitals, no punctuation. It seemed to be all one sentence.

Was this a joke? Was some friend teasing him with a note written in a disguised hand?

"My lord," he read, "out of the love I bear to some of your friends I have a care for your preservation therefore I would advise you as you tender your life to devise some excuse to shift of your attendance at this Parliament for God and man hath concurred to punish the wickedness of this time and think not lightly of this advertisement but retire yourself into your country where you may expect the event in safety for though there be no appearance of any stir yet I say they shall receive a terrible blow this Parliament and yet they shall not see who hurts them."

Lord Mounteagle read the letter through twice. Then he left the table and rode at once to Whitehall. At the palace he showed the warning message to the king's minister.

"I'm not greatly surprised," said Cecil. "I've been hearing rumors of a rising among the Catholics. Let us send for the Lord Chamberlain." Suddenly he turned to his caller. "You bring me this, Mounteagle, you, a Catholic?"

"I am a loyal Englishman first, sir."

When the Earl of Suffolk came the three talked earnestly together.

"The fifth of November—that gives us plenty of time.   Delay till as near the date set as possible.   Don't frighten the conspirators away.   Let us catch them red-handed!"

"Yes," agreed the Lord Chamberlain.   "If we let them proceed to the last point it will add to the value of the discovery."

All the public arrangements for the opening of Parliament went on.   Ministers of the crown too could keep a secret.   They made not a move that would let men suspect a plot, a grave danger threatening king and nation. But certain phrases in the anonymous letter to Lord Mounteagle set them thinking.   A terrible blow—should not see who hurts them. Terrible—could it be gunpowder?

On the third of November James I came up to London from a hunting trip.   Cecil showed him the letter.   Did they tell him their suspicions?   Or did the king justly claim afterwards that it was he who guessed the meaning of that warning message?   At any rate orders were given to the Lord Chamberlain to search thoroughly the cellars under Parliament House.

Mounteagle and the Earl of Suffolk went to Westminster the next afternoon. Pretending to be searching for some goods of the king's left in Whynyard's keeping, they knocked at the cellar entrance. Guy Fawkes opened the door. The Lord Chamberlain glanced in, saw the piles of fagots and asked to whom they belonged.

"To Mr. Percy whose servant I am."

"Well, your master has laid in a good supply."

That was all. As soon as the two gentlemen had gone Guy Fawkes set off at once to tell the conspirators they were discovered. But the sanguine Percy would not be alarmed. When night came he walked round Westminster with his servant to prove to him that all was peaceful. The fuse was laid. Fawkes had only to fire the train and escape as planned.

But at two in the morning came a party of soldiers commanded by Sir Thomas Knevett, a magistrate of Westminster. To the silent, dark cellar they made their way. On the stairs they met the tall figure of Fawkes, lantern in hand.

"Surrender! In the king's name!"

Fawkes stared at them.

"Seize him!" commanded Sir Thomas. "Now search him."

In his pockets they found slow matches and pieces of touchwood.

"Oh," cried the prisoner, "if you had but taken me inside! I'd have blown you all up— the house, myself, and all!"

"Search through the cellars," ordered Sir Thomas.

With drawn swords his men cleared away the fagots of wood and found the thirty-six barrels of gunpowder with a fuse ready laid to set them off.

Bound hand and foot Guy Fawkes was carried off to Whitehall and led into the royal bedchamber. There he was questioned by king and ministers.

"How could you have the heart to destroy so many innocent people?" asked James.

"Desperate diseases need desperate remedies," was the answer.

Frankly Fawkes told the details of the gunpowder plot. But tell the names of the conspirators he would not; no, not even when they took him to the Tower and day after day by the king's special order, tortured him to make him speak.

By noon on the fifth of November news of the discovery in the cellar of Parliament House was all over London. Catholics and Protestants were aghast at this plot of a dozen men, which had come so near succeeding.

When early that morning the conspirators learned of Guy's arrest they mounted their horses and rode at top speed out of London. Cecil's order to close the gates came just too late. But contrary to every expectation of the plotters the government found loyal friends on all sides. Watchmen told by what road a group of men had left the city. Villagers along the highways to the west reported a party of horsemen riding so fast that two of them had tossed aside their cloaks. Soon soldiers and sheriffs were hot on the trail of the fugitives.

"Once people know of the plot," Catesby had said over and over, "Catholics everywhere will rise to aid us. We'll soon have a big army."

At each turn of the road came reinforcements not for them, but for their pursuers.

An ever increasing number of citizens, Catholic and Protestant alike, joined the officers of the king.

Through Warwickshire and Worcestershire rode the conspirators heading for Wales. They knew that they were closely followed, that escape was becoming impossible. At a lonely country house on the border of Staffordshire they stopped to rest.

They were wet through in a storm. Their damp powder was put before the fire to dry. A hot coal fell into it and the mass blew up. The men's faces were scorched and blackened by this explosion. Some of them were badly burned. One was blinded.

"It is God's judgment," they cried, "for the deed we planned!"

Soon the house was surrounded. The conspirators refused to surrender. In the desperate fight that followed Catesby and three others were slain. The rest were taken prisoner and carried down to London for trial.

The hall at Westminster was crowded when the case was heard. King and Prince of Wales, lords and bishops and members of the

House of Commons, all the intended victims of the gunpowder plot were present.

"Guilty!" was the announcement of the court, heard with shouts of exultation by the crowds of people outside the building.

Catch the fellows red-handed, the ministers had planned, and make them an example to the populace. Through the streets of London the eight conspirators were led to execution. From the great crowds came not a word of sympathy, only cries of hatred and scorn.

Some in St. Paul's Churchyard and some at Westminster in front of Parliament House, the plotters were hanged and quartered. The bells of London rang and bonfires blazed to show the people's thanksgiving that the traitors had failed in their design.

Catesby schemed out the gunpowder plot and was the real leader. But his name is scarcely known. Always Guy Fawkes has been considered its most important actor. His lantern is preserved in the library at Oxford. And in the lieutenant's room at the Tower you can still see a marble slab with an inscription telling of Fawkes' examination there and of the narrow escape of the rulers of

England. For all these years it is Guy Fawkes who has been burned in effigy on the fifth of November. And at the opening of each session of Parliament the Yeomen of the Guard march through the vaults in search of gunpowder.

PEWTER PLATES AND HEAPING PLATTERS

Thanksgiving!

How much the very word says! Thanksgiving—you can feel the frosty air and the cold wind. You can see the bare trees against the gray sky. You can see the logs blazing on the hearth. You can hear the talk of travelers returning home for the day, the gay chatter and laughter of the young folks going to Grandfather's for this holiday.

Thanksgiving—guests coming up the walk with cheery greetings. There are the smiling faces of cousins, aunts and uncles, full of gratitude and love. Thanksgiving—the one word tells it all.

Thanksgiving Day! Church in the morning, where members of all the different congregations meet for a union service. It is the one day of the year when they do this. Fitting it is that they give thanks, most fitting that they give thanks together.

After church comes the great event of the day, the Thanksgiving dinner. Vary as its details may in different years, in different sections of our country, it has always these fundamentals—turkey, cranberry sauce, and to crown the feast, the golden pumpkin pie. Sniff, sniff! Didn't you smell them early this morning during the half hour of baking; smell the spices and the pumpkin and that special odor of flaky piecrust? Didn't you get the savor of the turkey when with flushed face Grandmother herself opened the oven door to baste it with the rich, brown juice? Turkey and cranberry sauce and pumpkin pie! A full table, not because we want so much to eat, but to symbolize the treasures of the generous earth! But turkey, cranberry sauce, pumpkin pie—it's a feast for the gods! a feast for Thanksgiving Day!

Though this November holiday is peculiarly American, the custom of celebrating the end of the harvest is not new. In England it was a famous holiday as far back as Alfred the Great's time. And before there was an England the Romans had a harvest festival in honor of Ceres, a festival as old as the reign of Romulus. And before them the Greek

women of Athens went each November in a
gaily bedecked procession to the temple of
Demeter to give her thanks for the bountiful
harvest with which she had blessed the land.
And before Greece the Jewish people had a
similar festival at Jerusalem, called the feast
of tabernacles. You can read of it in Plutarch, in Nehemiah and Judges, and in the
still older book of Exodus where Moses gives
directions for its observance.

But these celebrations of the end of harvest
lacked something of our American Thanksgiving. A full three centuries old is this holiday. It was in December of 1621 that Governor Bradford announced that first day of
rejoicing and thanksgiving in the little colony
of Plymouth.

Not quite a year had passed since the *May-
flower* anchored in the harbor of that rocky
coast. What a year it had been—a year
of hardships in a new land, a year of hunger
and cold, of fear and constant sickness! The
supply of food grew less and less. At one
time all but seven persons in the colony were
ill. For the sick there was not the right kind
of food. Week by week Pilgrims had died
till six and forty graves were dug on the bluff

overlooking the bay; dug there and left level with the ground around, without any mound of earth, without marking stones, lest the savage red men learn how few the colonists were in numbers.

But with the spring even the disheartened among the Pilgrims took heart once more. Go back to England, three thousand miles away? Never! Here they could worship God in their own way. Here they were free men.

With stout hearts, with steadfast faith the fifty colonists began to sow their seed. Twenty acres of corn they put in, six of barley and six of peas. Without ceasing they cared for these fields. They watched the growth of their crops anxiously. Well they knew that their lives depended on a full harvest.

Spring and summer days flew by. The land was blessed with showers and sunshine. Autumn came and dressed the woods in gorgeous colors—gold and crimson and brown. Their crops stood ready for the gathering. They reaped the fruit of their labors and housed it carefully for the winter.

In December Governor Bradford looked

abroad on the little colony. Seven houses he counted, and four for community use. He gazed over the empty fields—the twenty acres whose golden shocks of corn had stood so close together, yielding a harvest such as old England never knew; the barley too had been a successful crop; but the peas had been planted too late and though they came up and bloomed, the hot summer sun withered the vines and parched them in the blossom.

"Yes," said the governor to himself, "after the 'starving time' we've lived through there's ample food on hand now for all of us. There's a peck of meal a week for each person, and since the harvest there's the same amount of Indian corn. We can face the winter and the future with lighter hearts. There'll be no second 'starving time'!"

If a man counted only hardships, Bradford's thought went on, this first year in Plymouth had a goodly number. If he counted only blessings there were many, many. How could he best bring this truth home to his people?

"We have fasted together," he said in suggesting his plan. "Now let us feast together.

Let us have a special day to give thanks for all the goodness of God. He has remembered us. We will remember Him."

The date was set for the thirteenth of the month.

"Let us invite our friends, the chief Massasoit and some of his braves," suggested Elder Brewster.

A runner went to Mount Hope to take the invitation to the Indians. Four men were sent fowling and such good fortune attended their shooting that in one day they got wild turkeys, partridges and wood pigeons— enough to last the whole colony almost a week.

As soon as the plan for the feast day was announced the women set to work. Indeed it was a big task for the five of them, with a few young girls to help. There were pumpkin pies to be made and baked; turkeys to be plucked and dressed and stuffed with beechnuts; fish from the bay to be cleaned and broiled; barleybread and cornbread to be made; and many another good thing to be prepared. Busy, busy were the women and girls of Plymouth for days beforehand.

Early in the morning of the thirteenth,

shortly after Captain Standish had fired off the sunrise gun, there came a great shout from the woods. Another shout, a shriek and a wild whoop! Through the trees came a long line of Indians—the chief Massasoit and ninety of his braves. In their best dress they came, with flourish of tomahawks in honor of this feast day of their friends, the pale faces. Some of them had wide bands of black paint on their faces. Some had feathers stuck in their long, straight, black hair. Some wore the furry coat of a wildcat hanging from their shoulders. Some wore deerskins.

With the governor Captain Standish went to meet them. Were they surprised at the number? Were they dismayed at thought of the food necessary for ninety visitors? Courteously they received their Indian guests.

Presently the beat of a drum announced morning prayers. Every day began with this brief service. How much more important on this feast day! The red men looked on quietly, listening reverently while the stern, grave Pilgrims prayed to the Great Spirit.

Then came breakfast—clam chowder with biscuit, hasty pudding served with butter and treacle; for milk they had none in Plymouth.

At the north end of the little village colonists and visitors assembled.

"Military exercises under the direction of Captain Miles Standish," announced the governor.

The trumpets sounded. From the fort came the roll of drums. Down the hill in soldierly array marched the regiment of Plymouth—a regiment of twenty men. Over them floated the flag of England.

March and countermarch, wheel and turn, right about face—through all the maneuvers Standish put his men that morning. Frequently they discharged their muskets. Once in answer there came a great roar from the four cannon of the fort.

The red men danced, acted out stories and played games with the children. The colonists sang their songs. A target was set up and the soldiers fired at it. The Indians standing in closer shot at it with their bows and arrows. There was a friendly contest to see which side would make the larger score.

Meanwhile Mistress Brewster and Mistress Winslow with the three other women of the colony were hard at work. Remember Allerton and Mary Chilton, Priscilla and Desire and the younger girls helped as they could. Back and forth to the kitchen they went countless times, bearing pewter plates and heaping platters of good things to eat. At last dinner was announced.

What a meal that was, served at the long tables under the leafless trees! There were clams and scallops; wild turkey with Priscilla Mullins' famous dressing of beechnuts; dumplings made of barley flour; pigeon pasty; bowls of salad wreathed with autumn leaves; baskets of wild grapes and plums; and the crown of every Thanksgiving dinner, the golden pumpkin pie.

Did the Indians surmise that their presence made extra work for the women of Plymouth? Did they wish to bring something of their own for the feast? The brother of Massasoit offered to lead a hunting party into the woods to look for deer. His braves knew well their favorite haunts. It would not take long.

"Yes, go," said Governor Bradford.

The next morning back came the red men with five deer. One they roasted whole. The others were cut up into steaks and smaller pieces for venison pie.

For two days more the feasting went on.

Between English colonists and fierce Indians there was hearty fellowship and good will. Peace had been established on a firm foundation. Without such a peace the Pilgrims would never have won a footing on that bleak coast. Without it Plymouth could never have lived through that first year. It was these friendly savages who told the newcomers how to use shad to fertilize their fields, when to plant corn—"as soon as the oak leaves are as big as a mouse's ear—" and where to find wild fruits and berries. Much was owing to the red men. Thrice welcome to the colony's feast day!

This is the story of that first Thanksgiving in far-away 1621. Since then in Plymouth, in the Massachusetts colony there have been many such festivals. Sometimes there were two a year, if some special event made the leaders appoint a day of thanks and rejoicing. When hard times came and the outlook was disheartening they skipped a year. But from one generation to another in New England Thanksgiving has gone on and on.

The rest of the country was slow to adopt this beautiful custom. Here and there a governor proclaimed a day of thanksgiving

for his state. But it was not permanent.
There was no general celebration.

Soon after the middle of the nineteenth century a New England woman went from Boston to Philadelphia, to become editor of the
famous magazine called *Godey's Lady's Book*.
She was greatly impressed by the fact that in
Pennsylvania, and in other states as well,
Thanksgiving Day was not observed. To her
mind this was a state of affairs to be altered.
At once she set to work.

She wrote to the governor of each state asking him to appoint a day of thanksgiving and
suggesting the last Thursday in November.
Some governors met her request. Some ignored it. The next year she wrote again, and
the next and the next. By 1859 Thanksgiving Day was observed in all but two states.

Then came the civil war. There was no
time for a celebration when every one was occupied in work for the soldiers. No one had
heart for a festival when hearts were saddened
everywhere. But with the coming of peace
President Johnson proclaimed a day of
thanksgiving for the whole nation, in November of 1865. State after state followed.

Since that year America has kept this holiday, proclaimed anew with each November by governors and president. The reasons for giving thanks in 1621 have remained to this day, with many others added. It is a day when the people recognize all the blessings of God and His goodness to our land, a day to give thanks for bountiful, golden harvests, for peace and prosperity, for the general welfare, a day for prayer and rejoicing.

Turkey and cranberry sauce and pumpkin pie!

What a tantalizing odor when the kitchen door is opened for a moment!

There are voices from the gate and steps on the frosty path.   More guests are coming. For this is Thanksgiving Day!

THE BIRTHDAY OF THE KING

Nearly two thousand years ago when Rome was mistress of the world the emperor Cæsar Augustus ordered that every subject in his dominions should pay a tax. Each man must pay this not in the town where he happened to be living, but in the place from which his family had come. All through the great Roman empire people were traveling to their old homes.

From the land of Galilee a carpenter who lived in Nazareth journeyed south sixty miles and more to a village called Bethlehem, the city of David. For this man who was named Joseph and his wife Mary were descendants of the royal family of David, greatest of the Jewish kings.

Though their ancestor was so important a person Joseph and Mary were not rich. They were poor and humble folk. They found that many others had come to Bethlehem to pay the

305

Roman tax.   The little village was crowded. The inn had more guests than it could accommodate.   There was no room anywhere.   In a stable the couple from Nazareth found shelter.   Perhaps it was merely a cave hollowed out of the soft chalk rock, such as is found to this day in that land and used for the horses and camels of caravans.

Some months before an angel had come to Mary to give her a wonderful message—that she was chosen to be the mother of Jesus, the redeemer for whom all the Jews were looking, the one who should save the people from their sins.   He would be the son of God.   He would be also the son of man.   He would have the throne of David and of his kingdom there should be no end.   Awed by these words, yet very happy too, Mary had bowed her head and said humbly, "I am the handmaid of the Lord."

And now it was time for all that the angel had said to come true.   There in the city of David a son was born to Mary.   She wrapped him in swaddling clothes, the linen bands that eastern mothers wound round and round the body of a little baby.   Then she laid him in a manger.

How bright her eyes must have been as she gazed lovingly upon him and remembered the angel's message! Already the promise seemed to be coming true. Here they were, come to pay the Roman tax, in David's very city. A king to sit on a throne? This baby had no cradle save the manger of cattle. To wear fine clothes embroidered with jewels? This baby had only swaddling bands. To reign forever in a kingdom without end? David had ruled, but his realm had been divided, then conquered. This baby with the glorious future had no courtiers to rejoice at his birth.

On the slopes of the hills about Bethlehem were flocks of sheep. Night and day the shepherds watched them just as long ago in that very place David had watched the sheep of his father. In the night sky came a sudden brightness. Around the men shone a glory that was like the glory of the Lord. An angel came down to them.

"Fear not," he said seeing how frightened they were, "I bring you good tidings, news of great joy for you and for all the people. This night the Saviour is born in David's town of Bethlehem. This is how you may know him —he is wrapped in swaddling clothes. And here is a second sign—he is lying in a manger."

As the dazed shepherds looked and listened many angels joined the one who had brought this joyful message.

"Glory to God," the men heard them say, "glory to God and peace on earth and good will to all mankind."

At that hour the priests at the temple of Janus in Rome closed the gates of the building, the great gates that always stood open in time of war and were closed at the coming of peace. For the second time in history there was peace throughout the Roman Empire, peace throughout the world for the birthday of this baby.

The shepherds stared at one another. They looked up at the angels who were disappearing from sight. "Glory to God," sounded the last of their song of praise. The bright light was gone, the glory that had shone around them.

"Come, come," one cried, "let's go to Bethlehem and see the child who is born there."

"Yes," the others answered, "let us go, go at once."

In haste they ran down the slope, with those

words of praise still sounding in their ears, and through the streets of Bethlehem. No use to ask their way, no use to inquire at the crowded inn. They sought out a stable as the angel had directed. And there they found Mary and in the manger the baby Jesus. The shepherds sang a song of praise and glory to God, for what they saw and heard that night.

Other visitors too came seeking this child, wise men from the east who had seen a strange, new star and followed it, in order to worship the newborn king of the Jews. Across desert lands, over plains and hilly country the star had guided them. But when they neared Jerusalem it disappeared in the fog. They must needs ask their way.

"Where," they questioned, "is the king whose star we saw, the king to whom we would pay homage?"

The chief priests and Jewish scribes quoted from the prophecies which had been made more than seven hundred years before and answered, "In Bethlehem of Judea."

As the wise men turned to the south to journey six miles further to the city of David, the star again went before them. How they rejoiced! How steadily they gazed at it and followed exactly till it came to rest—not over a palace or a beautiful home, but over a stable! Could this be the right place? There was the star, their star they called it after all those days of its guidance, standing still now and shining brightly.

Into the stable went the wise men from the east. They saw Mary and the baby Jesus. They knelt down and worshiped him. Opening their treasures they gave him rich presents —frankincense and myrrh and gold.

Almost two thousand years ago, according to this legend, Joseph and Mary journeyed from Nazareth to Bethlehem and took shelter in a stable. Almost two thousand years ago Christ was born in David's city as the prophets had foretold. All these years His birthday has has been celebrated. It is the world's greatest holiday, observed in more countries, dear to more peoples than any other.

In the account of the birth of Jesus in the Bible there's not one word or phrase to show what time of year it was. There's nothing to indicate the month or season even, save that the shepherds were watching their flocks all night;

and this they did for ten months or more in that eastern land.

In the early Christian church the celebration of Christ's birth was held at many different dates—on the sixth of January, near the end of March, in April or May, in September and October, and more than one day in December. About the year 340 the pope fixed upon the twenty-fifth of December and that date has been accepted ever since.

But December holidays, a time of mirth and gladness and rejoicing for all the people, were known long before the year 340 or the year 1. Like others of our festivals the Christmas celebration was partly adapted from the pagans—Romans, Saxons, Scandinavians. It honored the mightiest event in the history of Christendom, but it was overlaid upon heathen festivals.

Many people kept holidays when the sun reached its southern limit and wheeled back toward the north announcing the end of winter. The Greeks had such a festival in honor of their god Bacchus, giving themselves up to songs and dances and revels. The ancient Romans kept this festival in honor of Saturn, feasting for seven days that often ended in rioting and disorder. The German tribes kept it and called it the feast of the twelve nights, in honor of the victory of the sungod and the south wind over winter and the storm-god, destroyers of life.

In the merriment and jollity that mark our holidays at Christmas survive the revels of the Greeks, the Saturnalia, the celebration of the twelve nights. The Christmas candles, the lights we have everywhere, we use because the Romans gave presents of wax candles. The Yule log that is brought in with such ceremony, welcomed with song and sport, burned on our hearths and for good luck a piece kept for next year's lighting, is a remnant of the great log which the Scandinavians kindled in honor of their god Thor. Boxing Day in England when poor people go the rounds with a Christmas box and ask for money is another survival. The Romans hung up earthen boxes with a hole for slipping in gifts of money for the rural festivals.

These old pagan celebrations the early church adapted, changing from the birth of the sun to the birth of the Son. This was merely giving them a new name but keeping the heathen date and customs. For more than a thousand years Christmas was a religious celebration only. Try as it would the church could not make the day popular. Gradually it transferred to the twenty-fifth of December celebrations that had belonged to Martinmas and St. Andrew's day in November, to the festival of St. Nicholas on December sixth, and to the feast of the wise men in January. Combining all these with Christmas, little by little the day became popular. It became the great festival of the year for children and the best time in all the calendar for the giving of gifts.

Who was St. Nicholas that a change in his festival should change Christmas? Not much is known of him. He lived in Asia Minor in the fourth century. Though he was the son of rich parents he would not accept their wealth for himself, but used it for the poor. He was still a young man when he was elected bishop. Old pictures show him dressed in embroidered red robes lined with soft, white fur, with cross and jewelled mitre and staff.

In many countries he is the special saint of schoolboys. No other saint had so many churches, chapels, altars dedicated to him as had Nicholas. Before the Reformation there were three hundred and seventy-six churches in England named for him.   Many boys were christened after him.   The name was as common as Mary among girls.   What is your name? asked the catechism.   N or M, was the answer printed, these initials chosen because Nicholas and Mary were the commonest names in England.

The reason for this is told in the legend of three schoolboys who were murdered by a treacherous innkeeper.   Their bodies he cut up and salted away in a pickling tub.   Nicholas made the sign of the cross over the cask and behold! the three boys arose alive and well.   The good saint gave them back to their mother.   The wicked landlord was stoned to death.

Nor was Nicholas the patron saint of boys exclusively.   In his parish was a nobleman who had three daughters.   Once he had been rich.   He lost his wealth and was so poor that he could not give them any dowry—the sum of money a bride brought from her parents, with which the young couple could start housekeeping.   The father feared he must send his daughters out as servants, but sorrow made him put off telling them.

At last the story came to the ears of the good

bishop. A shame, thought he, that this should happen in a Christian country! One night when the daughters slept and their father watched and wept, Nicholas took a handful of gold and tied it up in a silken purse. How could he give it without making himself known? While he stood hesitating the moon shone out from a bank of clouds and showed him an open window. In through the casement he tossed the gold. At the father's feet it fell. Thus the first daughter had her dowry and could marry the man she loved.

Soon after this Nicholas tossed another purse of gold pieces in at the poor nobleman's window. The second daughter was provided for. The father's curiosity was aroused. Who had come to his aid so generously? He wanted to thank his unknown helper. He determined to keep watch every night.

For the third time the good bishop went to the noble's house. Just as he was lifting his arm the father seized the skirt of his robe crying, "Oh sir, flee not away that I may see and know thee!" Then flinging himself at the bishop's feet he cried out, "Oh Nicholas, thou servant of God, is it thou? Why seek to hide thyself?"

"Promise that you tell no man what has occurred," was the saint's answer.

Artists often used to represent Nicholas with three golden balls, the three purses of gold he threw in at the window. Some Italian bankers who had chosen Nicholas as their patron saint were the first to lend money on pledges. Their three golden balls became the sign of the pawnbroker.

Thus St. Nicholas came to be associated with the giving of presents as were the three wise men from the east. And though in Italy the sixth of January is the time for gifts, and in France New Year's day and in Belgium St. Nicholas's day, most of the world sends its presents for the twenty-fifth of December.

Thor and Bacchus and Saturn, the bishop Nicholas and the wise men from the east have all contributed to our Christmas celebration. Many of our customs were not ours originally, but are frankly borrowed from other lands. So long is the list of these borrowings, could one tell them all, that it shows as perhaps no other holiday does how truly are we a composite nation made up from the whole world.

Our greeting of "Merry Christmas" comes from medieval England. The evergreens and mistletoe which deck houses and churches for the holidays date back to the time of the Druids. In solemn procession the priests went to cut the mistletoe, clad in white robes and carrying golden sickles. It was supposed to keep away witches and people paid the Druids large sums for a piece to have as a charm. Other greens they used in their houses to shelter the kind woodland spirits who found their favorite haunts bare in the winter.

The glossy branches of holly were used, says an old legend of the Danes, for the crown of thorns with which the Roman soldiers mocked the Saviour, and its bright red berries are the drops of blood that fell from His brow. The apples that every household has in abundance at Christmas time are what is left of the old myth of Iduna, the Norse goddess of youth and health, who gave them to the gods to keep them ever young. The gilded nuts and balls are a symbol of the sun.

Our Christmas carols date far, far back to the song of the angels that first Christmas Eve. The use of greeting cards, a custom so popular of late years, is rather modern. It began in England in 1846 when Sir Henry Cole sent the first ones to his friends. They were the

size of small visiting cards with a spray of holly or mistletoe and the compliments of the day.
As an experiment a printer published a thous-
and cards and—sold them all!

From Belgium we borrowed the Christmas
stocking, at least the germ of the idea. The
children there put their shoes—wooden shoes,
china shoes sold in the shops for this special
purpose, or everyday leather boots polished
extra well—close to the hearth. In them they
put oats, carrots, or potato peelings, a feast
for the white horse of St. Nicholas.

In the morning they find that a strange
thing has happened. All the furniture is
topsy-turvy. The food in the shoes is gone.
In its place are sweetmeats and little gifts for
good boys and girls, bits of coal and birch rods
for the naughty ones. On his way to America
St. Nicholas changed his white horse for a
team of reindeer, and the shoe custom was
altered to stockings.

Not one day do we have at Christmas, but a
full week of vacation and merrymaking.
"The holy days" the early church called them,
for each day of the fortnight had a special service—Christmas Eve and Christmas Day, St.
Stephen's, St. John's, and so on to Epiphany,

the feast of the wise men. Greeks and
Romans and Scandinavians celebrated for a
week or more. We still follow the old medieval custom of watching the old year out and
welcoming the new year with the ringing of
bells. But New Year's, the turning of a fresh
page in the book of life, is by no means a new
celebration. It dates back to 3000 B. C. at
Babylon.

All our holiday customs, you see, are borrowed, even the Christmas tree. That comes
from Germany if indeed it doesn't come from
very much farther back, from the sacred ash
tree which the Scandinavians thought grew at
the roots of the world.

There's an old legend that we owe the Christmas tree to Martin Luther who was once jour-
neying homeward on the twenty-fourth of December through a snow-covered country under
a glittering starlit sky. He was entranced by
the glorious mystery of the stars. He tried to
explain to his wife and children how beautiful
a sight it was. He went out into the garden,
cut down a little fir tree, dragged it into the
nursery and put some candles into its branches.
He lighted them and behold! the first Christmas tree! Each year Luther dressed such a

tree for his children to enjoy. His neighbors borrowed the idea and little by little it spread over all Germany.

It was the marriage of Queen Victoria to a German prince that took the Christmas tree to England. When their oldest child, the Princess Victoria, was five years old her father set up a tree on Christmas Eve, German fashion, in the nursery at Windsor Castle. It was about eight feet high with the figure of an angel with outstretched wings at its top. It had dozens of wax tapers and candies of all kinds, gilt gingerbread, fancy cakes, toys and dolls. This set the style in Great Britain. The next year a Christmas tree blazed and twinkled in every household.

The tree came to America however before it went into England. German settlers brought the custom with them. Christmas trees were lighted and enjoyed wherever there was a little group from Hamburg or Berlin. New Englanders were slow to take up such a practise. Their ancestors had protested earnestly, bitterly against such celebrations. So fierce an assault on Christmas they made that during the Commonwealth the day was driven from the land by act of Parliament. Indeed for more than twenty years it was against the law to celebrate Christmas in Massachusetts.

The day is named for the Christ-child, His mass. We celebrate to remember His birthday and honor Him. Why then do we have Santa Claus and from what country does he come?

From Holland and our Dutch friends whose patron saint is Nicholas. See how the name came to be: St. Nicholas, St. Nicholaus, Niclaes, San Claus—there you are, Santa Claus! Long has America been his home, for he came to New York, New Amsterdam it was called then, with the earliest of the Dutch settlers. The ship which carried them to the new world bore a figurehead of St. Niclaes. Their first church was named for Nicholas and he was the patron saint of the new town on Manhattan island.

Romans, Teutons, wise men from the east and humble shepherds, French and Belgians, Greeks and Dutch, men of every land have helped build up our Christmas customs. In return we must make our celebration all-inclusive, a season of the year when every one shares in the fun and jollity, in the greens and gifts, in the true holiday spirit. With bright red ribbons and holly, with dolls and soldiers and tin horns, with apples and golden oranges, it's easy to keep Christmas.   But you can't keep it alone.   It is only kept by being shared.

READING LIST

If you are interested in these holidays and their heroes and want to learn more about them, read—

ROBERT E. LEE

Barnes: Son of Light Horse Harry
Bradford: Lee the American (by a northerner)
Faris: Makers of Our History, chapter 16
Hill: On the Trail of Grant and Lee
Lee: Recollections and Letters of General Robert E. Lee (by his son)
Page: Robert E. Lee, the Southerner (by a Virginian)

THE FEAST OF LANTERNS

Doolittle: Social Life of the Chinese, II, 34–38
Giles: Chinese Sketches, 108–111
Gray: China, chapter 11
Headland: Home Life in China, chapter 14
Miller: Little People of Asia, 323–325
Van Bergen: Story of China, part II, chapter 10

Abraham Lincoln

Bolton: Poor Boys Who Became Famous, 342–367
Browne: Every-day Life of Lincoln
Lodge and Roosevelt: Hero Tales from American History, 323–335
Sparks: Men Who Made the Nation, chapter 12
Tarbell: Boy Scouts' Life of Lincoln
Whitlock: Life of Abraham Lincoln

St. Valentine

Brand: Popular Antiquities of Great Britain, I, 53–62
Chambers: Book of Days, Feb. 14
Denton: Holiday Facts and Fancies, chapter 3
Hone: Every-day Book, I, 215–231
Patten: Year's Festivals, chapter 3
Urlin: Festivals, Holy Days and Saints' Days, 34–37

George Washington

Baldwin: Four Great Americans, 9–68
Brooks: True Story of George Washington
Dana: Makers of America, chapter 2
Gordy: American Leaders and Heroes, chapters 10, 16
Hapgood: George Washington
Irving and Fiske: Washington and His Country

Japanese Festivals

Ayrton: Child Life in Japan, 64–67
Bacon: Japanese Girls and Women, 28–31, 362-364
Blaisdell-Dalrymple: Umé San in Japan
Fraser: Letters from Japan, I, 297–304, II, 235–252
Huntingdon: Asia, a Geography Reader, chapter 18
Kelman: Children of Japan, chapter 13

St. Patrick

Chenoweth: Stories of the Saints, chapter 4
Flood: Ireland, its Saints and Scholars, chapter 2
Joyce: Wonders of Ireland, 5–17, 136–152
Mannix: Patron Saints, III, chapter 2
St. Patrick, Apostle of Ireland
Steedman: Our Island Saints, chapter 4

Lexington Day

Bacon: Historic Pilgrimages in New England, 332–399
Brooks: Century Book of the American Revolution, 17–54
Coffin: Boys of '76, chapter 1
Moses: Paul Revere, the Torch Bearer of the Revolution

326 THE WORLD'S HOLIDAYS

Harper's Monthly 85:165 (1892): How the Declaration was Received in the Old Thirteen

Higginson: Young Folks' History of the United States, chapter 20

Lodge: Story of the Revolution, chapter 7

Merwin: Thomas Jefferson, chapter 4

Morse: Thomas Jefferson, 23-35

JAN HUS

Hodges: Saints and Heroes to the End of the Middle Ages, 248-257

Kryshanovskaya: Torch-bearers of Bohemia

Lutzow: Bohemia, an Historical Sketch, 91-107

Maurice: Bohemia, 175-220

Monroe: Bohemia and the Cechs, chapter 4

Schwarze: John Hus, the Martyr of Bohemia

BASTILLE DAY

Carlyle: French Revolution, book V, chapters 4-7

Farmer: History of the French Revolution, 149-170

Kirkland: Short History of France, chapter 29

Marshall: History of France, chapter 78

Morris: Historical Tales—French, 269-274

Price: Stories from French History, chapters 20-24

SIMON BOLIVAR

Couch: Roll Call of Honour, chapter 1
Dawson: South American Republics, II
Johnston: World Patriots, chapter 2
Olcott: Good Stories for Great Birthdays, 352-392
Sanderson: Hero Patriots of the Nineteenth Century, chapter 4
Sherwell: Simon Bolivar

The Star-spangled Banner

Columbia Historical Society 22:207 (1919): Dr. William Beanes
Key-Smith: Francis Scott Key
Marine: British Invasion of Maryland, 166–169, 182–190
Patriotism and the Flag, chapter 4
Pickett: Literary Hearthstones of Dixie, 175–198
Scharf: History of Maryland, III, 116–122

UNITED ITALY

Bayley: Making of Modern Italy
Birkhead: Heroes of Modern Europe, chapters 16, 17
Garibaldi: Autobiography

Sedgwick: Short History of Italy, chapters 37–38

Standing: Guerilla Leaders of the World, chapter 9

Trevelyan: Short History of the Italian People, chapters 27–30

CHRISTOPHER COLUMBUS

Bolton: Famous Voyagers and Explorers, chapter 1

Johnson: World's Discoverers, chapters 3–7

Lennes and Phillips: Story of Columbus

McMurry: Pioneers on Land and Sea, chapter 7

Moores: Story of Christopher Columbus

Seelye: Story of Columbus

THE GUNPOWDER PLOT

Ainsworth: Guy Fawkes

Brooke-Hunt: Prisoners of the Tower of London, 253–263

Creighton: Stories from English History, chapter 37

Dickens: Child's History of England, chapter 32

Gardiner: What the Gunpowder Plot Was

Marshall: An Island Story, chapter 74

THANKSGIVING

Carver: Sketches of New England, chapter 2

Earle: Customs and Fashions in Old New England, chapter 9
Love: Fast and Thanksgiving Days of New England, chapters 5, 27
Magazine of American History 8:757 (1882): Origin of Thanksgiving Day
Magazine of American History 14:556 (1885): Thanksgiving Day, Past and Present
Tittle: Colonial Holidays 52–73
Wiggin and Smith: Story Hour, 107–114

CHRISTMAS

Hodges: When the King Came, 1–39
Jameson: Sacred and Legendary Art, II, 450–465
McKnight: St. Nicholas
Pringle and Urann: Yule-Tide in Many Lands
Walsh: Story of Santa Klaus
Warren: Holidays, chapters 1–8

REFERENCE INDEX

THE END